I0465621

BUYING YOUR DREAM HOME

Save Money

Avoid Mistakes

Robert Borneman

Copyright © 2019

Robert Borneman

All Rights Reserved

This Work is Dedicated to my wife, Joy.

Thanks for a lifetime of love and friendship!

TABLE OF CONTENTS

PROLOGUE

There Is More to Know,
Than There Is to Do!

CONGRATULATIONS! You have already taken the first step towards creating a brighter future for yourself. Owning a home is not only the American dream, it is a significant financial investment. My goal is to help you make a sound investment without making costly mistakes or missing opportunities to buy the right home for you.

Admittedly there is a lot of content within this book to absorb, and it may seem scary or overwhelming at times for the first-time home buyer. I coined the phrase *"There is more to know, than there is to do"* because it is important to understand while you are reading this book that you will learn a lot about potential issues you may never encounter. This is clearly not the same thing as experiencing all the challenges or setbacks that you could potentially encounter, or which are discussed in this book.

I spent more than two years compiling notes and preparing this book from my experiences of buying and selling homes for more than 40 years, so that in a few hours I could make you aware of things that *could* happen but ***should not*** happen if you use the knowledge offered here. During this time, I have encountered hundreds of different situations and managed many properties. The hope is, the knowledge provided within these pages will save you a tremendous amount of time, money, and potential stress or heartache. One of the secrets to success lies within understanding the mistakes you want to avoid making.

**Inaction at the appropriate time,
can be more valuable than action.**

This book is also designed to acquaint you with some of the language and common practices of the real estate industry. Every chapter includes subheadings to make future reference easier. I employed this method, so you do not necessarily have to read the chapters in order. Terms and phrases or *trade jargon* are noted in italics, often followed by a definition or the vernacular use of the term or phrase. Tables are provided to demonstrate the math behind the explanation of financial concepts, offering a clearer perspective of ways to save money.

Understanding the underlying math of borrowing, even though it is a difficult topic for some, will allow you to make better financial decisions. It is time to take charge of your own financial destiny! Wise investing in your own home may also allow you to accumulate significant wealth, while enjoying some tax benefits. As a result, you will improve your personal lifestyle.

When you begin searching for a home armed with the knowledge found in this book and your own local research, you will learn a lot about the market in your area. Understanding your marketplace, lining up your finances and knowing what type of home you are seeking to acquire will allow you to strike quickly when the right opportunity for you arises. I have also included some tips on how to sell a property when the time comes or if you decide to trade up.

In instances where math calculations are used, I often work with a base price for a property of $100,000. The reason for this is so you can very easily apply a multiplier, even just in your head, to extrapolate how the example would relate to the real-world numbers of your own transaction. This means if you are looking at a $250,000 property you would use a multiplier of 2.5 ($250,000 divided by the example value of $100,000 = 2.5).

As an example: using a 5% interest rate without compounding or adjusting for principal reductions, the cost of carrying a $100,000 loan would be $5,000 for one year.

Therefore, on a $250,000 loan the interest will be $12,500 ($5,000 x 2.5) and for an $800,000 loan it would be $40,000 ($5,000 x 8).

For lower valued properties such as one with a $50,000 cost the multiplier becomes a fraction of the $100,000 example, ($50,000 divided by $100,000) becomes one half, expressed as .5 and the interest in this example would be $2,500 ($5,000 x .5). This simplified method allows you to calculate the actual numbers in a transaction you are considering very easily, and I think you will find it helpful in my examples.

I truly hope you find some ideas here that motivate you or assist you in becoming a happy homeowner. Wishing you all the best!

CHAPTER 1
WHY BUY REAL ESTATE?

CONGRATULATIONS!

If you are considering purchasing your dream home, this will probably be the largest personal financial commitment you have ever made!

CREATING WEALTH
A primary reason it is so hard for the average individual to get ahead financially is the tax burden we live with every day. April 15th is settlement day with the Internal Revenue Service, but every week the government shares in your hard-earned income by taking a portion of it to use for the greater good. Every dollar you earn creates a debt you owe to our government.

STOP paying as much in taxes as you are now by sheltering some of your income through real estate ownership. Wealthy people work much harder at preserving their incomes than lower income people. They can afford tax professionals and attorneys to work for them. They use the tax laws to their advantage and utilize tax planning strategies to minimize what they must pay in income taxes. You can too!

Here you will become exposed to the concepts of creating and using tax deductions to your advantage, as well as learning how to defer income and the accumulation of assets from being taxed at current tax rates. Interest on your mortgage and your real estate taxes are tax deductible on your federal tax return, although each State or the Federal Government may change the limits or rules on what is taxable within their jurisdiction. Capital gains can be rolled into your next home, tax free, when you satisfy the requirements to do so.

Because our tax laws allow you to *defer* or delay the payment of income taxes for an infinite amount of time on certain real estate transactions, you might not ever have to pay the taxes on accumulated wealth from your real estate holdings during your lifetime!

HOW TO DO IT
This book will provide you with specific "how to" methods and tips for buying a home, while maximizing the financial benefits of ownership. A

primary goal is to always work smart, not hard. You will learn to leverage your dollars, making them work harder for you. The passing of time will benefit you as your equity and income builds over the coming years.

The three methods of building wealth through real estate investing for homeowners are the concepts of *Equity Build Up*, *Appreciation* and in some instances *Income* or *Cash Flow* from renting a portion of a property. If you are a qualified investor, you may also be able to take advantage of *Depreciation* as a tax benefit. Proper maximization in each of these areas will drive your net worth exponentially higher. Each of these benefits may be extremely valuable on their own merits, but in total, with the value of *managed risk*, they make owning a home the clearest path to building wealth I know of.

If none of the above has convinced you that real estate is a great investment, then consider the fact that the housing market crisis, which has passed for many Americans, is over. The market hit rock bottom and has already shown healthy gains in some areas. Many market indicators say appreciation has returned! I can also tell you, based upon my own recent experiences while shopping for additional investment properties, that we are now seeing upward price movement, marking the beginning of a new market cycle of growth. I believe the current upward momentum of housing prices will continue for some time, maximizing your opportunity for appreciation.

There are also some intangible benefits of owning real estate that can be enjoyed, which include *pride of ownership* and the extremely rewarding ability to accumulate wealth and succeed on your own merits.

I have included a systematic format for the preparation, calculations and action items required to acquire a property. The broad strokes are outlined in the chapter titles and bold headings are included within each chapter for topics, to make future reference easier.

WHY BUY NOW?

Prices have started rising steadily in many areas since the recent collapse of the housing market. Since then, many of the vacant and bank owned properties have been rehabilitated and worked their way back into the mainstream housing market.

Interest rates are rising again and undervalued inventory on the market is now shrinking in many areas. NOW is the time to buy, because the perfect storm of low interest rates, availability of *inventory* (houses) and bargain prices exist. I suspect this will probably not last through the next decade.

Because interest rates are expected to rise, you can borrow money much more economically now than you will be able to in the future if this holds true. There are still bargains remaining in the market that have not been liquidated since the housing market crash. This trifecta of events is compelling on a case by case basis, but in sum, I think we are seeing an opportunity for returns on your investment that may not occur again for quite some time.

SWEAT EQUITY

Sweat equity, named for the fruits of your own labor, or with the help of family and friends is created when you do the repair work and make improvements to your home instead of hiring a contractor to do them. This is a great way to add value to your home and have some bonding time with others. Distressed properties and fixer-uppers create entry level purchase prices in most areas.

These types of properties may provide an opportunity to buy a larger home or some extra land for the same budget a move-in condition property would allow. If you can forego the look and feel of new construction or a home that needs very little work, a fixer upper may be for you.

When looking for a house that has sweat equity potential, be sure you can handle the type of renovations that will be required on your own. Avoid houses that will require significant work to be performed by contractors, so your costs do not run out of control.

Will you want to do most or all the work before you move in, or will you have a multi-year plan to upgrade different aspects of the house over time? Be sure that the condition of a property is not so bad that you will not be able to get a mortgage.

YOU ARE NOT BUYING A HOME
You are not buying a home, you are buying a house. This is the mindset you should adopt when shopping for a house which will ultimately become your home. It's great to be excited and emotional, and you should be, but your buying decisions MUST be rooted in sound financial planning.

Making intelligent decisions instead of emotional ones can help you buy a home you can be comfortable in for many years or a lifetime rather than becoming burdened by a money pit.

It is what you do with a house along with the love, experiences and memories shared under a roof that make a house a home. For most people, purchasing their first home is a very significant financial transaction. Therefore, when we seek to acquire a home, we must set out to buy a house built upon a financial foundation not just a concrete one. Avoiding being blinded by emotion will save many people future heartache because of a failure to do the due diligence and the proper math before signing on the proverbial dotted line.

Owning your own HOME is the American Dream. It is true that we may all have different definitions of what that home might look like, but most of us will probably think of our dream home as a single-family home with three-bedrooms, a garage, maybe a basement that could be finished some day and a white picket fence! For others it could be a condo or studio style apartment they will take ownership of. The good news is, for every taste and type of individual there is, there is a unique home waiting for you to find it!

INVESTMENT

Because you expect to live in the home you are buying, you probably will not categorize its purchase as an investment like you would with stocks or bonds. The truth is, it is an investment, which hopefully will be the best investment you ever make. There is another important distinction between this purchase and most others you have made through your life. You are now about to purchase an asset that provides tax benefits and can appreciate. Unlike new motor vehicles and most other purchases that typically lose their value over time, or *depreciate*, real estate can *appreciate*, and grow in value significantly.

CHAPTER 2
WEALTH BUILDING

As each mortgage payment is made, a percentage of principal is paid off (assuming you took a traditionally amortized loan, not an interest only loan with a balloon payment). Your mortgage statement will show the principal that you have paid to date, which is your equity buildup in a property.

As an investor, I think of equity build up as a savings account that my tenants regularly contribute to on my behalf. As a homeowner, the same effect will be achieved with your own money. **As a mortgage matures and until it is eventually paid off, the amount of your equity build-up increases exponentially.** This happens because the interest due decreases on lower principal balances and more of your mortgage payment goes towards principal than it does in the earlier years. This is now your gain or profit in the form of additional equity in the property.

This is very important because your "savings account" will grow over the years. It is your money, which you can access if needed and will not be taxed if you withdraw it later through refinancing or establishing a home equity loan.

When you refinance, the money you borrow is tax free because it is accounted for as a loan or your capital being returned to you.

You can refinance repeatedly, whenever enough equity builds up from principal repayments or additional appreciation makes it worthwhile. Refinancing a property can also provide the down payment for another investment and the interest may be tax deductible.

If you have positive cash flow that you can afford to put back into a property, you can pay down the principle faster by making larger payments or an extra payment. If you can make thirteen payments a year (every four weeks) instead of monthly payments, the amount of interest you can save will be surprising because the savings are compounded over time. As interest rates rise, the value of paying a loan off quicker increases exponentially. The nice thing is that you are not obligated to make the extra payment, so you might make it some years and not others.

Chapter thirteen addresses the difference between making payments every four weeks (thirteen annual payments) or making twelve regular monthly payments, in detail so you can see how substantial the difference in the interest paid is. The concept of a bi-weekly mortgage is also discussed there.

Understand your extra payments become an illiquid investment, even though you may be able to re-borrow to use the funds or sell the property to remove all your equity at once. Because of the nature of real estate, it might take considerable time to free up your money. One way to avoid this would be to set up a home equity credit line, discussed in more detail in chapter eleven.

Eventually you will celebrate *mortgage burning day*, which is when your property becomes *free and clear* or *unencumbered*. Your principal, interest and escrow payments will no longer have to be paid to the bank. You will now also assume responsibility for paying the real estate taxes that were previously incorporated within your mortgage payment.

Remember: The tradeoff is short term loans build up more equity at a faster pace. Longer term loans can improve cash flow and provide larger tax deductions, but those deductions come at the cost of paying more interest to earn the deduction.

APPRECIATION
Appreciation is a source of passive income, increasing your net worth when the value of your property rises. Appreciation is arguably the most significant reason to invest in real estate. The prospect of appreciation can dramatically increase

your net worth as you hold a property over time. Appreciation is a result of rising replacement costs, renovations, sweat equity, increased demand for an area, inflation, and other market conditions. Appreciation, or a rise in value of your property over time, is another form of equity build up. This is one of the most powerful mechanisms by which you can accumulate **huge** tax deferred gains.

Because appreciation is not considered earned income, it is not taxable as it accrues, and it accumulates in the form of equity in a property until the property is sold.

Appreciation is deferred income, taxed at capital gain rates and not subject to payroll taxes and withholding tax requirements. After some accounting adjustments are made your net gain or loss on a property is calculated. If you incurred a loss it would be tax deductible and if you have a gain when you sell, the gain or profit will be considered a *capital gain* and be taxed as such. This is yet another advantage real estate ownership provides, because capital gains tax rates are usually much lower than they are for earned income. This distinction can result in untold dollars in tax savings commensurate with the size of the gain you have realized.

LEVERAGE

Appreciation also leverages the return on your investment. If you put 20% down on a $100,000 property and that property doubled in value over time, you would have achieved $100,000 in appreciation or a 500% gain on your investment. This is calculated by taking the $100,000 gain and dividing it by your $20,000 investment to achieve a gain of five times or 500% return on your investment. This is shown on the last line of the chart below.

If the same property increased only 10% or $10,000 in value, you would still have a 50% gain on your $20,000 down payment. This is shown on the top line of the chart below.

Appreciation, when calculated as a form of *R.O.I.* (*Return on Investment*), can easily surpass your equity build up in terms of value.

Table A:

$100,000 Value of House 20% Down = $20,000 Equity				
Appreciation	**New Value**	**Capital GAIN**	**R.O.I.**	**New Equity**
10% App	$110,000	$10,000	50%	$30,000
20% App	$120,000	$20,000	100%	$40,000
30% App	$130,000	$30,000	150%	$50,000
40% App	$140,000	$40,000	200%	$60,000
50% App	$150,000	$50,000	250%	$70,000
100% App	$200,000	$100,000	500%	$120,000

The figures in Table A demonstrate the total return from appreciation ONLY using the stated values. Because appreciation rates are not constant from year to year you will have a blending of rates of returns that can be calculated as a total rate of return at any given point in time.

In this example, and others throughout the book, it is easy to extrapolate the results for different values of properties by dividing the value of your property by $100,000 and using the result as a multiplier to see more personalized results. This may sound complicated, but it is not.

As an example, when using Table A, a $350,000 priced home would equate to a 3.5 multiplier ($350,000 divided by $100,000). Your down payment of 20% would now be $70,000 ($20,000 down in example times 3.5 = $70,000). Then following the numbers in the first row; 10% appreciation becomes $35,000 ($10,000 times 3.5 = $35,000) and your new value would be $385,000 ($350,000 purchase price + $35,000 appreciation). The $35,000 in appreciation is your gain and this also equals a 50% R.O.I. on the original $70,000 down payment in this example.

Your new equity would be $105,000 ($70,000 down payment plus $35,000 appreciation = $105,000). Note that these new values are simply 3.5 times the table values based on the 3.5

multiplier of the difference in price between a $350,000 property and a $100,000 property.

This is one reason I love math, it is consistent and logical, not emotional. As you scale your investments up in value, the rates of return and all other calculations remain the same, you just get larger results in gross dollars while the percentages remain unchanged.

ANNUAL RETURNS

Clearly these types of returns are not available from banks, bonds, or other interest-bearing investments. Also, other investments that might produce these types of returns have very high risk/reward ratios. Few offer the ability to be insured and have the security real estate offers.

In Table B, some examples of an annualized return with a 20% or $20,000 down payment on an original purchase price of $100,0000 are shown in a different format. This table shows the percentage of your gain, which is part of your profit, divided by the number of years it takes to make the gain for the amounts of $20,000, $50,000, and $100,000.

Your annual return can be calculated by dividing the *total return* or ROI from any line in table A by the number of years you have owned the property. The shorter the term of your ownership is, the greater the annualized return will be as a percentage of your total investment.

As an example, if you double your down payment of $20,000, making it $40,000, and it took 4 years to do this, then the $20,000 column below shows the 4 years equals a 25% return per year.

Table B:

$20,000 Gain	$50,000 Gain	$100,000 Gain
1 Year 100.00%	1 Year 250.00%	1 Year 500.00%
2 Years 50.00%	2 Years 125.00%	2 Years 250.00%
3 Years 33.00%	3 Years 83.33%	3 Years 166.67%
4 Years 25.00%	4 Years 62.50%	4 Years 125.00%
5 Years 20.00%	5 Years 50.00%	5 Years 100.00%
6 Years 16.76%	6 Years 41.66%	6 Years 83.33%
7 Years 14.29%	7 Years 35.71%	7 Years 71.43%
8 Years 12.50%	8 Years 31.25%	8 Years 62.50%
9 Years 11.11%	9 Years 27.78%	9 Years 55.55%
10 Years 10.00%	10 Years 25.00%	10 Years 50.00%

In Table B you can see the annualized returns appreciation can create. For this reason alone, investing while markets are appreciating makes tremendous sense. Recognizing the cycles of appreciation in real estate can allow you to make better investment decisions.

TAXES ON GAINS

Because the political climate changes, tax rates are always subject to change as well. Having the ability to select a time to sell that will benefit you is another way to defer your tax liability. If you have accumulated significant gains in years when tax rates were high and sold in a year when they were more favorable, your actual realized net gain would be even greater.

LIMITING FACTORS

There are some limiting factors that can slow, reduce, or eliminate your chances for appreciation. Many of these are discussed in the chapter five titled *Finding a Property*. Understanding the current and potential appreciation rates in an area will help you make more informed investment decisions. If the area you are seeking to purchase real estate in is experiencing depreciation in prices, then you would want to wait until the market finds a bottom and prices begin to recover somewhat before jumping in. The exception to this rule occurs if you are buying very cheaply and the potential for a gain despite flat or falling prices still exists.

Similarly, buying a property that has limited potential for appreciation for other reasons may hinder your overall investment returns. Examples of factors that can limit your growth would be things like purchasing a property that is too close to a heavy industrial complex or located near a business that emits obnoxious odors. Unusually heavy traffic areas or a location that is too remote can also limit appreciation and future resale potential. Similarly tract housing, with hundreds of similar houses in a development, offering no distinctions in appearance and floor plans, subject sellers to a buyers' market competing for price rather than value.

Continuous new construction, expanding outward in areas where land will be readily available for the near or long-term future, can limit appreciation significantly too. This happens when new home prices do not rise much because of *overbuilding* in relation to demand, thereby limiting the resale prices of pre-owned homes. The price spread between new homes and resales needs to be large enough to motivate buyers in a secondary market.

Builders also offer benefits and customization, often including financing options, that make it easier for potential home buyers to commit to a new home. Owning something that no one has lived in, that may have been made or customized for you and your taste, has tremendous value too.

CAPITAL IMPROVEMENTS
A capital improvement is a permanent addition or alteration to real property which adds value or prolongs the useful life of a property.

Capital improvements that you make on your property will add to the *cost basis* of your home for accounting purposes over time.

This means if you add an extension to your home, or complete major renovations, such as updating your kitchen or bathroom, then the value or a portion of the value of these types of investments will be credited in accounting terms to the cost of your home.

Keeping track of capital improvements is important because when you decide to sell, this will reduce the capital gain and therefore the tax you might owe on the difference between what you paid for the house and what you sold it for. These improvements will also add value to your property in the form of equity build up and allow you to ask a higher price when selling.

COST BASIS EXPLANATION

Basis or *cost basis* is the value of your home or other property used for tax purposes by the IRS. It is the sum of the purchase price you paid plus many of the closing costs, which your accountant will use to calculate your basis. Your closing statement lists many of the costs, but there may be others you paid for that are not listed here. Keep receipts for all your expenditures related to buying your home for your accountant to review. This is important because it can reduce your tax liability when you sell.

When it is time to sell, many of your selling expenses can also be added to your basis. Your adjusted basis is defined by the IRS as "Your adjusted basis is generally your cost in acquiring your home plus the cost of any capital improvements you made less casualty loss amounts and other decreases".

There is some good news if you have a capital gain when you sell a home that is your primary residence. You will be entitled to an exemption from taxes on the first $250,000 in profit you have made or $500,000 if you are married filing a joint tax return. You are entitled to take this deduction once every two years for as many times as you like.

INCOME FROM YOUR HOME

If you can rent a portion of your home or if you buy a two family, multi-family unit or a Mother/Daughter style home, then you will be able to collect some rental income. Rental income will surely defray the costs of maintaining your home. Bear in mind, the income you receive will be taxable adjusted by any deductions you may be entitled to.

IT ALL ADDS UP

The total sum you stand to make on your investment primarily comes from equity build up and appreciation, but there are many more benefits, some of which are outlined in the next chapter.

CHAPTER 3
MORE BENEFITS

RETIREMENT PLANNING
Another benefit real estate affords, is that it can be factored into your retirement plan since real estate may be passed from one generation to another. The way a property is *titled* or owned, from a legal perspective, will determine how the property is or may be passed on. Since corporations and trusts outlive people, there are many tax strategies that professional retirement planners or financial advisors can help you use to preserve more of the wealth you have accumulated in your lifetime. Reducing your estate tax burden to benefit your heirs is an important thing to consider as you accumulate significant assets. Proper planning will insure that your wishes can be brought to fruition.

The discussion of estate planning, trusts and wills is very complex and typically requires the attention of a specialist. The complexity and nature of estate planning often even goes beyond the experience of the average CPA. My brother, who is a financial planner has helped me immensely with tax guidance. He is a *tax architect* in the sense that he works within the tax codes, designing a pathway that taxpayers can follow to protect their assets from overly burdensome tax levies. There is a credit at the end of this book for his firm *Borneman & Associates* if you need guidance in this area.

Ultimately, even though no one likes to talk about it, estate planning should become a part of your end game plan. The goal here is to prevent your assets from being liquidated in an unfavorable manner. With proper planning, you can not only reap tax advantages, but also ensure some orderly transition of your assets after you have passed. Thinking ahead may address or avoid challenges to your will or even worse; leaving your heirs to deal with the potential consequences in the absence of a will.

LONG TERM FINANCING
Mortgages are readily available, and a generally cheap source of money compared to personal lines of credit, credit cards and other types of consumer financing. Mortgage rates are also much lower than commercial lending rates. The reason for this is your property is the collateral that protects a lender. Consumer financing and credit cards are only backed by a promise to pay and it is much harder for lenders to collect this type of bad debt, so they often resort to writing off bad debt as losses. Inflation also reduces the value of your dollars over the years so in essence you are paying

less for the money you borrowed during the later years of a loan in terms of your purchasing power.

COLLATERAL

In the same way the bank uses your property as collateral when you buy a home, you can also use it as you accumulate equity, or your mortgage is paid off. An important way to shelter your real estate asset base from taxes is to borrow against it instead of selling it. You can withdraw large sums of cash tax free by taking a loan against a property. You can also do this repeatedly as each mortgage is paid off or the value of a property increases significantly due to inflation.

As your equity in a property increases from equity build up or appreciation, the value of the property you can *pledge* as collateral also increases. Banks love real estate as collateral because it is an asset that reduces the risk they take when lending.

SECURITY

Another reason real estate is a great long-term investment, is that it can be insured. If you will have a mortgage, you will be required by the lender to have insurance. The lender will usually incorporate the premium in your monthly mortgage payments.

In the event of serious damage or total loss, rendering a property temporarily or permanently uninhabitable, you can be compensated rather than bearing the burden of a loss alone.

Even though your bank may remit the insurance premiums from your monthly mortgage payment to your insurer, it is your policy, not the banks. The bank is named as an *additional insured* and elects to pay the premium on your behalf, with your money they hold in escrow, so they know adequate coverage is always in place. In addition to knowing your coverage remains in place, the bank will also be notified of any changes to the policy or cancellations. As the policy holder, you should periodically review your coverage to confirm it aligns with your current needs.

You should also periodically check the amount of the insurance premium you are paying is a competitive rate in the marketplace. Even if you shopped well for the best price when selecting your policy, over time increases in rates may afford you a new opportunity to save with another insurer. Insurance markets change regularly as companies become more aggressive or less aggressive trying to gain your business. New companies enter the market while others leave, and underwriting guidelines are constantly changing.

In addition to being insurable, real estate is difficult to steal in the sense that it is impossible to physically move or hide. Yes, you can move a structure but not without being noticed, and the underlying parcel of land would retain its value. Aside from the rare fraudulent cases of an illegal transfer of ownership that make the news, real estate is secure. Unlike other valuable investments such as art, coins and many types of rare collectibles that can be easily transported or vanish without a trace, your real estate investment is a *fixed asset*, pun intended and will remain in place, literally for generations to come.

It is also worth noting that even in the rare fraudulent cases where a deed from a piece of real estate is transferred inappropriately, there is a paper trail that can be followed and undone. This type of recourse is extremely rare in instances for other types of investments where money or liquid assets are stolen and spent or dispersed in ways that prevent them from ever being identified or recovered.

INFLATION HEDGE
Inflation causes prices to rise and thereby creates appreciation. The advantage of being in the market vs. waiting to get into it, is that ownership creates a hedge against inflation. This is what I call the *treadmill effect*. Once you enter the market, your property value will adjust with inflation, allowing you to trade sideways in value for another property that has risen in price too,

because you have an equal investment, which has also appreciated similarly.

When you sit on the sidelines waiting for opportunities or to accumulate a larger down payment, rising prices could keep the investment you are looking for out of reach. A simple example is a $150,000 home appreciating at 5% a year, which will rise in value by $7,500 in one year. The longer you wait, the larger the down payment needed will become, making it more difficult to make the leap of faith to buy.

**Inflation is a primary reason
first time home buyer's
need to stop renting
and buy as quickly as possible.**

A "starter home" will get you into the market, allow you to build some equity, and provide a base to trade up from in the future. A starter home is also the best way to use your sweat equity fixing up a property, thereby achieving substantial equity build up plus appreciation and additional savings that can be used to trade up at any point in the future.

OWNER OCCUPANCY

As a homeowner you are an *owner occupant*, allowing you to use and enjoy an investment in a home compared to other asset classes such as stocks which provide little tangible benefit.

If you buy a multi-unit residential property and you use one of the units to live in, then you would also be an owner occupant. You can derive additional benefits in the form of lower living costs subsidized by tenants renting your other units that could cover some or all your expenses. It will probably be easier to obtain financing as well, since banks like it when you have a personal stake in a property when they are lending to you. If you pay yourself rent and use the money to pay the mortgage down, it will take exponentially less time to pay off your mortgage.

If you are thinking about becoming a landlord, please read my book *"Why Flip? Buy & Rent!"*. Although the math concepts and some other chapters are the same as I have outlined in this writing, you will find a wealth of information about how to prepare a property for tenants, how to select a tenant, leases, evictions and so much more that it will certainly be worth your time to read.

INTANGIBLE BENEFITS

As a home owner, you become part of a community. The mark of your success can be left in a community through the way you maintain your property. This can also be said about acquiring high profile, prestigious or historic properties as people in the area will come to know you for helping to preserve their neighborhoods.

PAYMENT OPTIONS
If you are financing, the challenge will be to minimize your costs and shop for the best rate. Banks and institutional lenders often offer attractive interest rates but build in a lot of other costs to make their money. If you have access to private funding, it is usually the cheapest and easiest way to get started.

Do not be lulled into thinking there is not much difference between a 4 or 5% interest rate. The 1% increment sounds minimal, but it will increase your interest costs by 25%. This is calculated by dividing the 1% by the 4% rate. See the table below for interest on a $100,000 loan for 15 and 30 years.

4% Interest Rate		5% Interest Rate	
15 years	30 years	15 years	30 years
$33,143.83	$71,869.51	$42,342.85	$93,255.78

On a 15-year loan the interest rate spread from 4% to 5% would cost you $9,199.02 more.
($42,342.85 minus $33,143.83)

On a 30-year loan the interest rate spread from 4% to 5% would cost you $21,386.27 more.
($93,255.78 minus $71,869.51)

The term of a loan also affects how much interest you pay and will create an even starker contrast than what the difference in interest rates does. For this reason, you will hear me say more than once in this book to use fifteen-year financing instead of thirty-year terms whenever you can to reduce your carrying costs.

Cash is King, or Queen for the ladies, and so if you are buying all cash, you should be seeking the biggest discount, since you can close more quickly and do not have to make your deal based on financing. Each strategy for purchasing a property provides different benefits.

GRIEVE YOUR TAXES OFTEN

File a *tax grievance* every year or use a firm to do it for you. Real estate taxes are usually assessed at the Town level, unless there is a sub level of government such as a Village that has established its own taxation in addition to that imposed by the Town. Filing a tax grievance is lodging a formal complaint or a challenge to the amount of real estate taxes assessed upon your property by your town or taxing authority.

Taxing authorities do not use a current market value or *fair market value* of your property to calculate your taxes due, instead they use an *assessed value*. Your assessed value represents a percentage of the fair market value as determined by the governing assessor's office. Your assessed value is then multiplied by a factor called a *millage rate*, which is used to calculate everyone's taxes. The millage rate multiplied by the assessed value will equal the taxes you are billed. The millage rate is the same for everyone, so by raising the millage rate, the taxing authority raises your taxes while your assessed value remains unchanged.

By grieving your taxes, you are challenging the assessed value, which you are attempting to reduce, by providing comparable examples of similar properties with lower taxes in your area or other information that would justify a lower assessed value.

The tax grievance process usually occurs in two parts, the first of which is a hearing with the taxing authority, where you will have the opportunity to present your case. The taxing authority will review the documents and the argument you provide, then decide as to whether you are entitled to a reduction in your assessed value. Contrary to myths you may have heard, this is not an opportunity for the taxing authority to raise your taxes; by law an assessor cannot raise your assessed value simply because you have filed a tax grievance. The assessor will only decide if your assessed value should remain the same or be reduced.

If you are not successful or satisfied with the results at this level, then you can bring your challenge to court where an arbitrator will decide if an adjustment is appropriate. If you prevail, your tax reduction will be paid retroactively for the period in which you filed, and you will reap the benefits of any reduction in your assessed value for years to come. Even as the millage rate increases for all property owners, you will always be taxed based on the lower assessment you have received.

If you use a company to grieve your taxes for you, which I do, they can research the taxes on surrounding and similar properties, sometimes within minutes, depending on the software they use and tell you if you have a chance at winning a reduction. They will also prepare the comparable property data, complete the paperwork, attend the hearings, and go to court on your behalf if necessary. All you need to do now is wait for the results. In return for doing this you will be charged a fee, commonly a third or half of the tax reduction the company earns for you, however you will still receive the benefit of any tax reduction in future years without additional cost or fees.

Grieve your taxes every year you are eligible to do so!

CHAPTER 4
USING A BROKER

I recommend using a real estate broker or agent, several in fact, when seeking to purchase a new home. Since brokers usually represent the seller, do not accept everything a broker tells you as Gospel; do your own research and math calculations to confirm what you are told. Brokers may also represent the buyer or both parties and they are obligated to disclose who they represent even though it may seem obvious. Since the seller pays the broker's commission from the proceeds of a sale, there is no cost to you for using one or more brokers' services. You can however, hire a broker to act on your behalf as a buyer.

The reason for using multiple brokers is more opportunities will come your way from cultivating these relationships. Some brokers are better at finding deals and some just work harder for you than others. It will not take long to find a few brokers you are comfortable with.

I think most people see a real estate broker's job as a relatively glamorous position. They get to show beautiful homes and make gigantic commissions. In some cases, this is true but in most cases across America there is a different truth.   Selling real estate is a time consuming, hand holding, often thankless job. Hundreds of hours are expended trying to acquire listings and showing properties that never result in a sale and therefore never result in a commission. This can add up to a lot of unpaid time. So yes, there needs to be a payday at some point for a broker to become successful or at least stay in the business.

As in every industry the good and the bad coexist. I have a lot of respect for brokers who aspire to be the best they can be in their profession and really work to fulfill their clients' needs.

TYPES OF AGENTS AND BROKERS

The terms real estate broker, broker, real estate agent or agent are used interchangeably in this book and by many people. From a buyer's or seller's perspective, a transaction should be seamless using either an agent or a broker. However, the titles of Agent and Broker are very different in legal meaning. This is evidenced by different licensing requirements for a broker's license and an agent's license often referred to as a salesperson's license. The differences also have important IRS distinctions as well.

The title real estate agent or real estate salesperson is a generic term that describes any licensed professional in the real estate industry. Licensing requirements do vary from state to state, but all states require applicants to take classes and pass a state exam to become licensed. Most states use the titles agents and brokers, yet other titles do exist. Licensed professionals are empowered to represent and negotiate on a buyer's or seller's behalf.

REAL ESTATE BROKER

Real Estate Brokers must have experience as an agent, then they must pursue additional education and pass a broker's exam to become licensed as a Broker. Brokers commonly own or operate real estate offices that hire real estate agents or salespeople to work for them, however, a broker can work solo and conduct their own transactions. Brokers may hold deposits and establish escrow accounts as needed for real estate transactions.

ASSOCIATE BROKER

An Associate Broker is a licensed broker who works under the auspices of another licensed broker.

REALTOR

The term *Realtor* is also commonly misused and misunderstood. It can be used generically, but when the term Realtor appears with the registered trademark, REALTOR®, the term is being used to signify or identify a member of the National Association of REALTORS®. As a member, one is presumably held to a higher authority and standard of care while practicing in their profession. A REALTOR® agrees to abide by and conduct themselves by the standards and code of ethics the Association puts forth.

SELLER'S AGENT

A selling agent or *Seller's Agent* works only for the seller and is usually the person you agree to let rent or sell your property. A seller's agent is also often called the *Listing Agent*. A seller's agent is the gatekeeper buyers must negotiate with and through. The selling agent will arrange showings and host *open houses*. Open houses reduce the need for appointments and are commonly used to show newly listed properties to other local brokers and people actively seeking to purchase a home. In a very narrow window of time, that might only be two hours or most of an afternoon, brokers can sometimes produce an offer from a buyer in one day. The homeowner is not usually present to preserve the broker's ability to negotiate on behalf of the seller.

The listing agent works with a seller to determine a proper asking price by providing *comps*, or comparable prices for similar homes that have recently sold in the area. The agent may suggest ways to prep a property for sale, so it will show better. Agents also prepare the listing, advertise the property, receive, and present offers, make appointments for appraisals and work with other parties to facilitate a deal.

BUYER'S AGENT

A *Buyer's Agent* represents the buyer only and will assist a buyer with finding a property. The buyer's agent will also negotiate a purchase price and assist the buyer as required until the closing is completed. A buyer's agent will sign a separate contract with a buyer for services rendered in addition to earning a piece of the sales commission that is paid by the seller at closing.

DUAL AGENCY

An agent can represent the buyer and seller at the same time, which is commonly known as a *dual agency*. A dual agency is legal in most states but must be disclosed to both parties. In New York, agents use a disclosure form that you must sign as acknowledgment of the dual agency.

ATTORNEYS AS BROKERS

In some states like New York, attorneys can become brokers without the practical experience of being an agent. This is because of the intense exposure to real estate law received when studying for and taking the bar exam to become an attorney.

HOW COMMISSIONS WORK

Under normal circumstances, when you are buying a property, you will not be paying the commission, the seller will. For purposes of understanding who gets paid and their relationship to you, here is how commissions are typically broken down for the most common combinations of agents and/or brokers involved in a transaction.

Brokers and agents do not earn a commission until and unless a transaction *closes*. A closing takes place at the point in time when the required documents are signed and the full purchase price changes hands. The process of closing is outlined in greater detail in chapter seventeen titled *The Closing*.

- Transaction with only one Broker representing buyer and seller.
    Broker = 100%

- Transaction with 2 Brokers = 50% to each Broker.
    Listing Broker = 50%
    Selling Broker = 50%

- Transaction with a Listing Broker and an agent from another office. The Selling

Agent will split half of the fee with the Broker from their office.

Listing Broker = 50%
Selling Agent = 25%,
Selling Broker = 25%

- Transaction with two Sales Agents (from different offices) and two Brokers.

Broker A = 25%
Broker B = 25%
Agent for Broker A = 25%
Agent for Broker B = 25%

- Transaction with two Sales Agents (from same office) with one Broker.

Broker = 50%
Listing Agent for Broker = 25%
Selling Agent for Broker = 25%

These are only guidelines that are subject to negotiation between brokers and agents. As depicted here, a broker can attain a 100% commission, but an agent cannot, because they are always working under a broker. If your listing agent sells the property, they also become the selling agent at the same time and will earn two parts of the full commission. In some instances, further splits can occur when additional agents or brokers become involved in a transaction.

At the closing, the full commission due can be paid to the broker or brokers that may distribute the funds as necessary to any agents that may have participated in the transaction.

CHAPTER 5
FINDING A PROPERTY

A wish list will help you and a broker eliminate houses that will not fit your needs and select houses for showings that do. A wish list should be composed of things you must have and things you would like to have, so it might look like this:

> A two-car garage
> 2 bedrooms minimum, 3 or 4 a plus
> Modern kitchen
>   (granite or stone counter tops preferred)
> Inground pool a must
> Fireplace if possible
> General good condition:
>   not looking to do a lot of work
> Painting, flooring, minor repairs OK
> Separate dining room (no eat in kitchen)
> Basement (can be unfinished)

A review of my sample list demonstrates how many properties a broker might remove from their list of houses to show you because they are now armed with information that will save you both time and effort in the shopping process. The longer and more detailed a wish list is, the more of a picture you are painting of what your dream home will look like. Obviously, everything is subject to change.

When I was shopping for my first house my wife did not want a Cape style home. She had grown up in one and wanted a change. We looked at quite a few houses that we rejected for different reasons, but an underlying criterion of "move in condition" started to surface. On one buying trip the broker said to us, I know you said you didn't want a Cape, but I have an expanded Cape with a beautiful sunroom extension that is immaculate, would you be willing to look at it?

We agreed to look and bought the house the same day, so hey, you never know!

FAIR HOUSING LAWS
A broker cannot always share everything they know about a neighborhood and may sometimes seem vague when you ask questions about a neighborhood. There are *Federal Fair Housing Laws* that prevent brokers from sharing certain types of information with you.

These laws are intended to prevent a practice known as *steering*, where brokers suggest or only show some neighborhoods and not others to buyers based on discriminatory grounds and this practice is illegal.

If you ask questions about a school, neighborhood, crime rate and so forth a broker should decline to answer those types of questions but should explain why.

If you want to know more about a neighborhood, you will have to do your own research to get the answers to these questions. Part of your research should include visits to a prospective property at different times of the day and different days of the week. Neighborhoods can take on a very different character at night and on weekends than they may have during working hours when most people are not home. A seemingly quiet neighborhood by day can morph into streets with lots of evening traffic, multiple cars in driveways, loud music, and people playing in the streets or loitering.

A visit to public parks and spaces, checking out the schools in person and camping out in the parking lot of a local grocery store for a while at different times of the day, will give you a sense of the neighborhood you are considering buying in. Crime statistics are easy to find by researching on the internet.

MULTIPLE LISTING SERVICES

Today, many brokers simply rely on the use of *Multiple Listing Services* or MLS, which is a large database of just about every property for sale. MLS allows many brokers to have access to the same properties at the same time. Therefore, exclusive listings are not as common as they used to be, but they certainly still exist. For this reason, if you work with multiple brokers, they may all try to show you the same properties. I usually let brokers know if I'm working with other brokers. Therefore, I ask what addresses they are planning to show me for the day before venturing out so as not to duplicate viewings.

EXCLUSIVE LISTINGS

Agents try to get sellers to commit to *exclusive listings* or *pocket listings* for initial offerings when an agent believes they can sell a property on their own. An exclusive listing allows a broker to offer a property to their clients first, in the hopes of selling it for a full commission. Brokers like exclusives, but they are not always in a seller's best interest.

Without the use of a multiple listing service or other brokers, the need to split the potential commission is eliminated. Exclusive listings also allow a broker and agents within the same office the opportunity to retain the full commission of a sale within their agency. Exclusive listing agreements are almost always memorialized in writing, to protect the agent's rights and be enforceable if a dispute arises.

Pocket listings are informal agreements with sellers, sometimes only sealed with a handshake, that place a property for sale without formally being listed for sale. This is one way to keep a potential sale "quiet" for any number of reasons, including shielding a client from public scrutiny when offering their residence for sale. High profile clients may not want their neighbors to know they need to sell. The dubious side of pocket listings is they can be misused to foster the illegal practice of steering individuals away from certain communities.

The value of an exclusive or pocket listing to a seller depends on how large or appropriate the broker's contact list is for a property, how they will market it and so forth. As a buyer, it does not matter if a property being offered for sale is an exclusive or pocket listing, or how the sales commission is split.

FOR SALE BY OWNER
Some owners will opt to try and sell their property using a listing site, newspaper ad or sign to find a buyer, but without using a broker. The primary reason is usually to save the commission, which can be a substantial amount of money. These types of offerings are called FSBO's, pronounced FISBO which is an acronym for *"For Sale By Owner"*. There are two distinct thought processes

when it comes to the concept of listing a property as *For Sale By Owner*.

Many sellers go it alone believing they can do a better job than a broker. For other sellers, their house may have been on the market too long or the seller has lost faith in one or more broker's ability to sell their home. Often sellers want a higher asking price than brokers feel is realistic based on the market, so they list on their own.

Many brokers shy away from showing houses they feel are overpriced, and they will try to discourage sellers from starting too high. This is only natural and sometimes proves to be in the seller's best interest overall. However, setting too low of a price to create a quick sale and quick commission at the seller's expense is a conflict of interest. One advantage of going it alone for a seller from the start is that you can always list with a broker later if you do not find success on your own.

There is also a belief among sellers, that buyers would rather deal directly with a seller. This statement is true for me as a buyer because I feel if the seller is saving the commission, then I can negotiate a better deal. When negotiating directly, I can usually do better at reducing the asking price with a seller, because a broker is a middleman trying to protect their commission. I also have had more success in obtaining information about a property, for better or for worse, that a broker may not divulge or even be aware of.

As you can see, listing an FSBO might not work out as well for the seller as they think. Remember in a deal, anything you and the other party agree upon can become part of your deal. When dealing directly with a seller the door is open to lots of negotiation tactics that may not work well with a broker as an intermediary. If a seller is going to give the commission away in a reduced price and forego the benefits of using a broker, it can benefit you.

Brokers can sometimes bring in an offer for much more than a seller might get on their own. This is true because brokers have advertising budgets to cross promote many properties all year long, so they develop a steady stream of buyers. Established brokers usually have an office that generates leads and have contacts for other potential buyers. Brokers also have web sites that may generate significant traffic and inquiries.

Brokers can pre-qualify buyers and assist them with figuring out how to finance a purchase, so they can afford the asking price. Remember the broker's commission is a percentage of the final sales price, so there is always an incentive for the broker to work at getting the maximum price for the seller.

The other side of a broker not being in a transaction is that as a buyer, you need to do a little extra due diligence when dealing directly with a seller as they have less obligation to disclose information a broker may be compelled to, such as lead paint disclosures.

When a property is being sold "as is", especially in a cash deal without a broker, a red flag is raised for me. Maybe the seller does not have CO's, there is a survey problem or some other issue lurking beneath the surface of a deal that the seller already knows will not pass muster with a bank or lending institution. If there are illegal additions, violations, or environmental problems a seller might not choose to act in good faith and make you aware of this information. A history of fire, criminal act, or other unusual circumstance are other examples of situations a seller may not want to disclose.

There is nothing wrong with someone trying to sell a property on their own, but sometimes sellers greatly underestimate the value a broker brings to the table. I believe in brokers because I have seen them create great deals for me.

FORECLOSURES
Properties that have been *foreclosed* upon or taken back by a bank, are also referred to as *REO's (Real*

Estate Owned). At some point banks will resell these properties, to recover the money they lent which was never repaid plus expenses. Expenses include the cost of securing and maintaining vacant properties as well as paying the taxes each year. These expenses are in addition to the costs of the actual foreclosure which could be $50,000 or more for a bank.

Contrary to some people's beliefs, banks do not want to take back properties because they are not in the real estate business. Holding vacant properties ties up capital in ways banking regulations and accounting practices do not favor banks. The current market value will determine if a bank will take a loss, break even or make a profit when it *liquidates* or sells a property it owns. Bear in mind the number of foreclosures will rise in poor markets as people lose jobs and real estate prices are falling, which will make it even harder for a bank to recoup the outstanding debt plus expenses.

Banks often resort to selling properties they have acquired through auctions which provide quick and definitive results. There are no contract negotiations and properties are usually sold "as is" without any contingencies. You may not even be able to see the interior of a property before bidding on it, which obviously creates an additional risk of liability and expense a buyer has to be willing to take.

The highest bidder determines what the bank will get for the property unless a *reserve* or *minimum bid* has been set. A reserve is a minimum price the auctioneer may accept regardless of what the *opening bid* may be, and a minimum bid would be the lowest starting bid a buyer could make.

A bank may also decide to list a property through a real estate broker in the traditional manner if there is a potential to achieve better results than the auction process may bring.

SHORT SALES

When a loan is in *arrears* and the bank has the option of declaring a *default* to bring a *foreclosure proceeding*, it may allow a homeowner to sell a property as a *short sale*. This means that the house can be sold for less than is owed to the bank and the bank will consider accepting offers which will result in the bank taking a loss. If this makes economic sense for the bank compared to the expenses of a foreclosure, a short sale will be approved, and a foreclosure sale will be avoided.

To be eligible for a short sale a homeowner must show the current sales value of a home is less than what is owed so there is no realistic way for the house to sell for enough money to pay the outstanding balance of a loan with the proceeds of a sale. This is referred to as being *underwater* on a mortgage, a term derived from *drowning in debt* no doubt. The homeowner must also demonstrate a *hardship* or inability to make the payments due on their home. There are many other rules and contingencies the bank requires when approving a short sale to be sure the homeowner is not simply trying to circumvent paying their debt.

For these reasons short sales can take much longer than traditional sales to be approved and processed, invariably resulting in a lot of offers being declined. Also consider that the bank is really looking to sell the property at the fair market value so there may not be a price benefit to a buyer, while the seller is being relieved of their debt. However, if you find the right property in a neighborhood you want to live in, you may be willing to jump through the hoops required to acquire a property being sold as a short sale.

IT IS TIME TO GO SHOPPING!
Where do you begin to find a home? You can work directly with a broker that will set appointments for you. You can also start with a web search on one of the many real estate listing sites. If you find a property of interest, you can contact the broker listed as the point of contact to arrange a viewing. There are also many "For sale by owner" web sites or listings you can search

through. I like to make several appointments in a day to make the most efficient use of my time when I go house hunting.

Most of these sites allow you to sort a search by price, zip code, number of bedrooms or bathrooms etc. The top price you enter in the price range search box can be a little higher than your actual maximum budget on the premise you should be able to negotiate into your comfort zone. If you want to become familiar with average prices for a three-bedroom home in an area, widen the search parameters and see where most selling prices fall. Understanding the highs, lows and median selling prices in a market will assist you in identifying a bargain or fair value when shopping for your home. Spending some time researching will educate you about common terms used in your area as well.

The lower end of your range can be any number, but if you start with zero you will find all the *fixer-uppers* in the neighborhood. I like to start with zero in a search anyway. It is a good idea to peruse these and become familiar with how cheap a property can be. Some of the lower priced homes are *tear-downs*, which as the term implies, need to be rebuilt from the foundation up. Therefore, this is more of an area for builders to find opportunities, than those of us that want to buy something closer to move in condition.

Unless you are willing to hire a contractor to do a major renovation or you can do it yourself, you will quickly find these ultra-low-price offerings need too much work to consider for the first-time home buyer.

BUY RIGHT

The process of shopping to buy right can be time consuming or a bargain could pop up on your first field trip. I have experienced both scenarios, but usually reject many homes before finding the right one. In addition to the many problems or potential pitfalls that exist with some of the properties you will pass on, sometimes your offers are rejected, or you must pass based on the math. Patience, research, and homework are necessary to find the right home and to identify a bargain when it appears.

When my mother went shopping for her second home, she looked at more than 200 homes. Every broker in town, and a few neighboring towns knew her. I had already moved out and my Mom had made a promise to my sister who was still living with Mom that they wouldn't buy a house unless they were both happy with it. So, each rejected their fair share along the way but eventually they found the perfect house for them and bought it. If you know what you want and persevere, you should be able to find it.

LOOK PAST COSMETICS

Poorly maintained homes exist in most communities for a variety of reasons. People age, they lose their jobs, medical issues arise, financial situations deteriorate from divorces and a myriad of other reasons affect an owner's ability to upkeep a property. Then of course there are some owners who just do not care to maintain their property even if they have the means to do so. Poorly maintained properties often provide opportunities to enter a better market than you might think you can afford and over time as you bring the property up to neighborhood standards you may be handsomely rewarded with the sweat equity you accrue.

CONVERTING A TWO BEDROOM HOME TO THREE BEDROOMS

If you are thinking about expanding a property you purchase to add one or more bedrooms, this is an area where some research may be required.

Expanding the size of a home can be a good investment and may provide significant lifestyle improvements. However, in some areas, to add a bedroom you may be required to apply for building permits or subjected to other requirements. In my area you must contact the Board of Health as well. My local Board of Health requires an upgrade to the septic system to accommodate additional square footage and occupancy. A septic system upgrade can cost a few thousand dollars that you will need to include in your budget. In addition to the renovation costs, increased real estate taxes and bringing the property up to the current code requirements, a building department inspection may uncover other issues. If so, these issues may have to be remedied and factored into your costs as well.

GARAGES

For purposes of resale, a basement and garage help tremendously, appealing to many home buyers seeking these amenities. In addition to the extra storage space and comfort a garage offers, there is a certain curb appeal from a garage that makes a house look much bigger as well. In areas that experience harsh weather; garages or carports can add value for a buyer. Will a one or two garage be on your wish list?

SIZE OF THE LOT

More land equals more taxes, so does a large lot have value to you? Sometimes the size of the land is significant enough to separate and sell or build on. Does extra room for a new pool, a garden, tennis or volleyball court, play set, trampoline, or other things interest you? Is the land wooded and maintenance free or will you be spending a lot of your time maintaining it instead of enjoying it?

NEW CONSTRUCTION

New home sellers set their prices based on current costs for construction. Bargains are rare, but the perks are key. There is a nice feeling associated with buying anything new. It smells different, feels different and it is pristine.

PREPARE FOR A BUYING TRIP

When you venture out on a house hunting excursion, whether it is to see one property, or you will be spending the entire day on the road shopping, there are several things you should do.

Bring a camera and note pad to document things that may need repair, require attention, or prompt future inquiries.

This will also help remind you of things to factor into your total purchase cost calculations or address in a negotiation later. If I am visiting multiple properties, I print out the listings and make my notes directly on each listing. The more houses you begin to visit, the more important this becomes, as you may need to refer to your note's weeks or even months later.

Unless you are looking at new homes, or well-maintained homes, you will find the condition of pre-owned homes can vary tremendously. If you are bargain shopping for fixer uppers or bank owned properties to employ your sweat equity, you may run into some homes in very poor condition. When planning these types of visits, it is a good idea to wear long pants and a long sleeve shirt.

The right clothes will help you avoid coming into direct contact with insects such as fleas or ticks and poison ivy, poison oak or other such things as you move about a property.

I always have a flashlight in my car in case a house has no power. A light is also helpful when going into any basement, crawl space or attic which can be very dark. Bringing a breathing mask in case mold is present and a bottle of water is a good idea if you are sensitive to dust. A tape measure may be useful as well.

THE NEIGHBORHOOD
While on your way to view a property, take notice of the surrounding areas and drive a mile or so in each direction to see if the neighborhood is consistent. If not, are there any red flags that need to be considered? When you arrive at the property take note of the level of *curb appeal* and determine if the house blends in with the neighboring properties. Also, remember to visit the property at different times to see if the feel of the neighborhood changes.

SCHOOL DISTRICTS

School districts may have dramatic influences on property values, property taxes and resale values of homes. The best rated school districts are highly desirable for people that place emphasis on a quality education for their children. If you are sending your kids to a private school or do not have children, you will still bear the cost of taxes associated with maintaining better school systems in a neighborhood.

THE WALK THROUGH

When doing your walk through a house, look at the bones of the house and the layout. The color of the paint is easy to change, and the furniture will be replaced, so do not let them influence your assessment of a house. You are probably looking to buy something that needs cosmetic attention, not significant renovations that take time and cost money, so adjust your standards accordingly. Remove emotion from your decision-making process. Is the space well planned or is there a lot of wasted space in hallways, nooks, or unusual storage areas?

Look at the ceilings; are they even? Is there evidence of current or previous leaks which would appear as stains, bubbling paint or sagging from the weight of accumulated water. If the source of the leak is rainwater, the water itself may be gone but there is usually a telltale sign left by any leak.

A thorough attic inspection will usually reveal the signs of a leak. Know that some leaks only occur when the wind and rain come from a specific direction or updraft conditions that allow water to enter under eaves. Therefore, a leak may not be active on every rainy day, but an experienced inspector should know where to look and what to look for.

Take a good look around the kitchen to determine if it will really suit your family's needs. Are you happy with the size of it? Are the type and quality of appliances going to meet the needs of your family? This is the room that is most expensive to update in a home so be sure the cabinets are in good condition. Do all appliances work? Is there enough counter space to work with?

Bathrooms follow the kitchen in the pecking order of cost to renovate so if you are not happy with the fixtures or condition of them, then factor that into the real cost of acquiring the house you are looking at. Is there a laundry room? Not every home has one and this could be costly to install new electric, plumbing and appliances even if you have the space to add one. Did you notice it wasn't on my sample wish list? Should it be on yours?

Look at the roof line. Is it straight or sagging? Is all the roofing material the same color or has some of it been replaced? If a shingled roof is redone, it is a common practice to go over the existing shingles with a new layer and there may be several layers of existing roofing. Building codes can limit the number of layers of roofing allowed. When considering the cost of replacing a roof, there is a substantial difference in labor and carting fees when several layers of roofing must be removed compared to going over an existing roof.

When ripping up shingles you also may find damage to the underlying structural materials. On shingled roofs the underlying plywood and occasionally some of the rafters need to be replaced. Common sense dictates that the older a home's construction is, the more important a detailed roofing inspection is. Are there gutters and leaders? Are they in good condition and do they direct rainwater away from the foundation of the house?

Landscaping improves the curb appeal of a home, so it adds value to a property in most instances. It also adds costs to maintain or consumes your free time if you are a do it yourself type of person. Assess the costs of maintenance including replacements of plants and shrubs that may not be healthy or you find unsightly. Include the cost of upgrades you might want to make for budgeting purposes.

When you uncover problems during the walk thru process categorize them as significant, which would require action for you to buy the home, or insignificant, which would be things you are willing to take care of yourself.

If there are a lot of insignificant issues you may want to factor that into your offer or if you are already in contract you may ask for a credit in the price you have agreed to pay. If there are items on your significant list, you should ask the seller if they are willing to fix these items before closing on the property. Based on the cost of significant repairs, you will decide if anything is a deal breaker for you.

If you haven't already eliminated a property during your walk through and there is a basement you should check it out. The condition of the basement can tell you quite a bit about a home. Hopefully everything looks normal but if it doesn't you will know it. Look for any signs of a water line from previous flooding. Do walls appear to be in reasonably good condition, free of substantial cracks? Are there any seriously abnormal odors. Basements are usually the home of heating and air conditioning systems. Do these systems look to be in reasonable condition? You don't have to be an expert, because if you make an offer you will have a professional check everything out. Sometimes you will realize right away that you will need to spend a significant amount of money to update a system in poor condition.

You can tell a lot about the care given to a property during a walk through and get a sense if the owner attends to problems as they arise or lets them fester based on the general condition and cleanliness of a home.

EUREKA!
Eventually, after researching, searching, and eliminating many properties because of the pitfalls you have learned about, you will find something you would like to buy! Now what? It is probably time to make an offer, but there are a few more potential pitfalls that you should be aware of before you should make that offer.

CHAPTER 6
THINGS TO KNOW BEFORE BUYING

Like everything else in life, every new venture comes with challenges and a learning curve. Hopefully, this book will allow you to learn from my experience to avoid the mistakes I made, and this chapter will prepare you for some other potential pitfalls that you will now be able to recognize for yourself.

ENVIRONMENTAL ISSUES
If a residential property is located near a commercial property, you must consider the impact that this will have on the level of your risk and ultimately the soundness of your potential investment. You want to be sure you are buying a home and not a headache. Because of the almost limitless exposure to liability in cleanup costs, I recommend staying away from any property that has environmental issues or has the potential to develop them during your ownership of a property.

When buying adjacent to or near a commercial property, remember commercial tenants change over time and so the nature of the business your neighbor might be operating is subject to change too. A business engaged in the use of petroleum products such as a gas station or repair center may have already developed an environmental problem that has not been detected yet.

Undetected acts of contamination can be significant if the contaminants seep into surrounding properties. Even if there is no contamination, the potential for it to occur in the future is greater in this type of commercial environment than in a purely residential neighborhood.

If a business or property has a history of using toxic chemicals, then this is a significant potential risk you should consider carefully before becoming their neighbor.

Phase One testing includes a site inspection, public record and property history searches, interviews with people knowledgeable about the area and a written report. A Phase One report plays an important role in determining if a Phase Two or Phase Three report should be performed. These types of inspections are common for commercial properties and may be necessary in some residential areas. If this is indicated, you may want to consider looking for another place to buy.

A Phase One report is substantial in size and usually contains a lot of standardized information about the area that is not specific to your property.

This information is helpful in educating you about your property and the surrounding area in ways like an appraisal for replacement value or a structural engineers report can. You may be able to use the contents of a report to renegotiate the agreed upon price based on details provided which you were not previously aware of. An additional price reduction at this point might also offset the cost of the inspection report as well.

Residential properties can develop environmental issues from something as simple as a leaking oil tank on the property that contaminates the ground. If you are planning to renovate, you may be required to have a licensed contractor remove and properly dispose of building materials made from asbestos. In homes built before 1975, materials commonly made from asbestos include flooring, ceiling tiles, roofing, exterior siding, shingles, and insulation.

Radon gas is a problem in many areas. Chemicals in sheetrock used throughout Florida now require removal or remediation of many newly built or recently renovated properties. Lead based paint was commonly used in homes prior to 1978 when it was banned. This type of paint is only problematic if there are visible signs of peeling and or chipping, which may require testing and to be professionally remedied if the damaged surfaces test positive for lead contamination.

Excessive mold may require hiring a professional to remove it safely. While issues that are small in nature and confined to a single property can often be resolved easily with relatively minimal expense, it is important to be aware of potential larger scale problems that have occurred in an area which you are seeking to live in. Underground plumes of pollution that spread within the aquifer can impact the value of homes in entire communities

I looked at a three-bedroom house that was being sold by a bank in an auction. A site inspection revealed a severely dented oil tank adjacent to the driveway that apparently was hit by a car, then pushed into the house. The house had minimal damage that could be easily repaired but a simple tapping on the oil tank revealed it was empty. So, a flag is raised, and the question arises; was all the oil used and the tank ran dry before being struck or was the tank empty because it leaked from being struck?

This was a bank owned property being auctioned off, so we asked the bank for a statement indicating there was no spill or they would bear the expense of a cleanup if required and they declined to do so. **Therefore, I bought a different house.** I was not willing to pay for a Phase One inspection only to <u>bid</u> on a property that I might not even be able to win, or worse, could win and have an environmental problem with no recourse. I might have made an offer to purchase the property if I had the option to withdraw based on the results of the report, but an auction is a final sale; buyer beware.

Researching a property for environmental purposes will tell you if there has ever been a cleanup conducted or if there is an outstanding violation. You will not be able to ascertain if there is a current problem unless you get an environmental impact inspection and review the report. While this is an additional cost, it would be a prudent one to make if you are considering purchasing a property near a potential contamination site.

Other environmental considerations beyond pollution and chemical spills can affect your quality of life and ultimately the resale value of your home. Issues such as excessively loud or continuous noise can be a deterrent. A street that is quiet by day can transform into a raucous crowded venue by night if you have a nightclub for a neighbor or are in a downtown area that has a healthy nightlife. Flashing lights, sirens from fire houses and other emergency response vehicles stationed nearby, railroad crossings and other things may make the price of a property attractive to buy but consider the effect they may have on you and your family. Fast food restaurants and other high traffic businesses can create traffic congestion or emanate cooking odors that permeate the surrounding area.

DEED RESTRICTIONS

Restrictions on your use of a property can be imposed within a deed, by a community association or by a local agency. Be aware that these can be positive or negative depending on your perspective. Beach or mooring rights for a boat that are granted to you in a deed might be a positive covenant. Whereas in some areas such as waterfront communities, you may not like the parking restrictions, beach access rules or other rules imposed by an association. Additionally, some towns require buffers or green areas to be maintained on your property.

You must inquire to become aware of potential restrictions that may be common in an area or a development to assess the impact they may have on your decision early in the process of shopping. Ask brokers to let you know if there are any deed or other restrictions on the properties they are showing you.

HOA'S

Home owner associations or HOA's are common in planned or gated communities, developed subdivisions and condominiums where common property or services are shared. This might include a club house, pool, tennis courts, golf course, security, parking areas and other amenities requiring management. An HOA is managed by a board elected each year by the residents of the community. Board members are usually residents of the community as well. The board is responsible for managing the property and will hire a property manager or use an outside service to manage the property.

The board also manages the finances of the property and enforces rules. The costs of maintenance for the common areas are covered by fees or assessments paid by the residents. A set of *bylaws* dictates the requirements for voting on and approving new rules, budgets, proposed expenses not in the budget, changes to the governing policy and so forth. In addition, associations usually have a set of *rules and regulations* addressing use of the facilities they maintain. Some rules and regulations will pertain to limiting or prohibiting certain types of conduct on the premises as well.

All homeowners residing within the jurisdiction of an association must abide by the existing rules. Anyone purchasing or renting within the community will also be subject to the rules as there is usually a covenant or restriction in deeds that grants the association this power. The rules are drafted by the board and voted upon by the residents. Violation of rules can land you in court and failure to pay monies owed to the association can result in eviction or foreclosure proceedings against a homeowner. Therefore, it is imperative you become familiar with the rules prior to entering into a contract to purchase a property in an HOA.

What kind of rules can an association set? Almost anything you can think of ranging from the hours the pool is open to what color you paint your house, to where you may park your car. Some rules may seem petty while others overbearing, but they were all approved at one time or another by the community. Any rule can be changed by a vote of the community as outlined in the bylaws or rules and regulations. You will find that most of the rules in any association are in place to improve the quality of life for all residents and preserve the resale values of the homes within the development.

EXPANDING COMMUNITIES

Whenever possible, investing in an area experiencing growth should be a plus, but sometimes it is not, and you need to be able to tell the difference.

Purchasing in areas experiencing population growth that outpaces housing availability helps fuel appreciation.

Be careful about buying in rural areas with new construction growth, which I would describe as *building rings.* Building rings are areas of new construction growth outside of which there is a perimeter of undeveloped land readily available to builders or already owned by builders that will be a continuous source of land for new construction. Over the years, the core or center of the ring ages and like growth rings on a tree, each year newer homes are built around the outer edges of an established community. In these areas, the chance for appreciation is limited to the cost of inflation for materials and not rising demand since the supply of new homes may not diminish for years to come.

I have even seen prices depreciate on resales within the growth rings because the new homes have not risen in price and buyers look for significant savings to buy used rather than new. Benefits offered in new construction will woo buyers and especially first-time home buyers, reducing the resale potential for the market.

This effect occurs in more rural environments than in cities and fully developed suburbs where *spot building* on individual lots that come onto the market or *tear downs* where old or dilapidated properties are torn down to build larger and/or more modern homes dominate the type of new construction. In these latter growth scenarios, the potential for huge increases in valuation are more likely.

CHAPTER 7
MAKING AN OFFER

When you have found a property that you would like to buy, you should make an offer. NEVER pay the asking price unless you have made an offer or attempted to negotiate, and the buyer is firm enough to walk away from the deal. If this fails and you still think the asking price is worth paying, then it is your call to make if you want to meet the asking price. Remember, the asking price is called an asking price for a reason, sellers and brokers expect and anticipate a reasonable amount of back and forth negotiating in every transaction. Do not be embarrassed or shy, this is an opportunity to save more money than you might imagine, so negotiate to the best of your ability.

THE ART OF NEGOTIATION
You can negotiate for almost anything as an add on, houses have been sold with cars, furniture, and other things as part of the deal. Everything except the proverbial death and taxes, both of which we are always trying to challenge, is negotiable. Negotiation is truly an art, which can be perfected. My first attorney taught me that **the strongest person in a negotiation is the one that can walk away from a deal**. Be that person.

When negotiating through a broker, it is much more difficult to ascertain the seller's true position than it is when negotiating face to face. This is one of the reasons brokers like to keep buyers and sellers separated. Sellers either talk too much and give in too easily to pressure from a buyer or the opposite happens, and they get insulted by offers they think are lowball or become offended by comments from buyers that they perceive to be a negative reflection upon their home.

As a buyer, I believe your ability to live without a deal gives you the upper hand in a negotiation. It does not mean you must walk away if you do not get everything you want, but it will allow you to retain control of negotiations, ultimately achieving much better results than you started with. The fact that you can exercise the option to walk away whenever you choose is very comforting. Negotiate from a position of strength but be wise in working towards attainable results or know your middle ground to settle on before entering discussions.

Since a seller typically sets the price and terms for a deal, the buyer is usually the one to open a negotiation unless they choose to pay full freight and agree to the asking price. Failing to negotiate is the weak way out in a transaction and often costs buyers more than they need to spend. A seller's need to negotiate arises from the need to make an intelligent *counter offer* if there is flexibility in the price and terms that were proposed. Factors such as how long a property has been for sale and how much interest there has been within a reasonable period, combined with the sellers need to sell, all play a part in a seller's decision when considering an offer.

The buyer on the other hand holds the money that the seller wants. A buyer's success results from using a combination of understanding psychology and physiology to identify, interpret and employ the signals the seller transmits during a negotiation. Understanding a few things about the person you are negotiating with will often help you make a better deal for yourself instead of achieving average results or making no deal at all.

COUNTER OFFERS

Often a seller will receive an offer that is less than their asking price and the offer may even be substantially lower than the minimum price they were hoping to receive. In these cases, instead of immediately rejecting a low offer, the seller can make a *counter offer* in an amount that falls between the asking and offered prices. This process may receive an immediate or delayed response from the buyer but now a negotiation has opened. This is where a seller's broker can earn their fee, bringing the buyer back up in price to a more palatable strike price.

The offer and counter offer cycle could continue for several rounds with both parties negotiating in good faith to make a deal from different perspectives on the value of a property. The decision to strike a deal is ultimately the sellers, who sometimes decides to walk away, meet the buyer in the middle or eventually settle for less than they are happy with to make a deal.

Remember everything is negotiable once a bargaining session begins, other things such as the timing of a transaction, what's included in the sale, items to be repaired and so on can become part of the negotiation. Offers and counteroffers may be subject to things such as inspections, appraisals, certificates of occupancy, attorney review etc.

BE PERSONABLE

The first step in any negotiation should not be an offer, but rather to start a dialogue with the seller. This conversation you strike up is really a fact-finding mission for you, which will hopefully prompt more questions to assist you in learning about the acquisition you are considering. The goal in a discussion is to endear the seller to you and to open doors, never close them or paint yourself into a corner so to say. Do not make demands or ultimatums that will kill a deal if the seller cannot meet them unless you are ready to walk away.

Sellers are not necessarily good negotiators, so they can easily become frustrated, which will cloud their decision-making ability. Remember for many sellers this can be the largest financial transaction they may make in their lifetime too. When working directly with a seller, do not be rude and do not make disparaging comments about a house that may have been the seller's home for many years. Derogatory comments may very well be taken personally by a homeowner.

Sellers can be finicky and may opt to sell to someone else they feel will "take care of" their property, whatever that means to them. They may also consider the impact selling to you will have on their neighbors. Even though this thought process may not seem logical from your perspective, emotions control the decision-making process for many people. This is one time I have found the expression "money talks" doesn't always ring true. Sellers have been known to take less money from a buyer they like, than selling to a perceived outsider. Your goal is to help them come to a palatable settlement, that benefits you both, which is not necessarily the one the seller originally had in mind.

Ask open ended questions and get the seller to talk about themselves, then ask why they are selling. **The more the seller talks about themselves the more they will like you.** Yes, this is true, so let them talk, you never know what you will learn. The more they like you, the more flexible, yielding, generous or forgiving they will become when you get down to the nitty gritty details of the deal. The goodwill you build here may also payoff in the remainder of the negotiation. A good relationship can also help you in the contract and closing process if you develop issues in performing your end of the bargain.

You always want to talk with the decision maker or at least have them present or immediately available by phone. Obviously, this is not always possible and many times you will have to deal with an intermediary, the broker. When this happens, just know a broker will try to negotiate against you and convince you to pay more because it is in both the broker's and the seller's best interests. Do not be lulled into believing the broker is working for you, no matter how nice they are.

As a licensed professional, agents and brokers are required to present your offer to the seller, regardless of their feelings about it. One of the great advantages to shopping for houses listed as "For sale the owner", is that you are almost always dealing with the decision maker in a one on one situation.

SELLER'S MOTIVATION

It helps to uncover a seller's true motivation for selling to make the best deal possible. Many things can motivate sellers other than money. Once you uncover a seller's true motivation, you will be able to negotiate based on the hot buttons that make a seller flexible. Within the context of understanding the seller's motivation you should also inquire as to what the seller will do with the money if you make a deal.

Sometimes knowing the reason, a seller is selling or what they will do with the proceeds opens a door that changes the direction of a negotiation. It also tells you about the level of urgency or timing the seller may be subjected to which might factor into your offer. As the amount of time a seller has remaining to complete a deal without incurring additional costs or consequences becomes smaller, the more leverage you will begin to achieve in a negotiation.

Dismiss preconceived notions. **The art of negotiating is forging a deal that two parties agree upon, nothing more and nothing less. Do not listen to naysayers who tell you it cannot be done.** Attempt to prove them wrong, as you have nothing to lose in failing to make a deal work.

BE A GOOD SPORT

I believe the art of negotiating is akin to a sport in the sense practice improves your skills and there is much satisfaction to be achieved from becoming better as you develop those skills. There is no need to kill your rival, only to beat them at the game. The journey can be like the thrill of a hunt and is as enthralling as the achievement of one's goal - a great deal.

ADD-ONS IN A NEGOTIATION

In addition to the deal at hand, opportunities to sweeten the deal may present themselves. These are considered add-ons that are negotiated into a deal. You are only limited by your creativity when it comes to adding on tangible or intangible benefits to make a deal work. When the negotiation for price has settled, or stalled, it is time to ask for the *sweeteners* that allow the seller to feel they are still getting a fair price but end up giving you significant extra value that lowers the net cost in your mind. Sweeteners are anything that a seller can give up which has value to a buyer, including furniture, draperies, generators, or a Porsche in the garage.

YOUR OFFER

Your offer should include the important terms of the deal and anything specific you may have negotiated with the seller such as:

"Time is of the essence, must close by Dec 31"
"Including all living room furniture"
"Including generator"
"Including 1964 Porsche 911"

If your offer is accepted, it may also be subject to certain requirements that will be spelled out when the contract is prepared. An example would be, if the seller has a date they must close by and they would bear unacceptable costs or other hardship, if a buyer fails to complete the deal in a timely manner, then they might say the deal is subject to closing by a specific date. Lawyers will insert language into the contract saying *time is of the essence*, which has a legal meaning that holds a buyer to a firm closing date. If the buyer fails to complete the transaction within the required period, the buyer may be subject to penalties or lose the deal and potentially their deposit too.

Under normal circumstances, closings are usually scheduled with an *on or about* date within a contract. Either party can request a 30-day extension and if both parties are agreeable, any duration of time extension is negotiable. Even when a situation becomes adversarial, an attorney can find plenty of ways or reasons to extend a closing date for several more weeks and sometimes months if necessary, to buy their clients more time to close. Therefore, the inclusion of a "time is of the essence" clause should be considered by a buyer or seller based on their personal circumstances.

Sometimes buyers try to insert what attorneys call *weasel clauses* into a deal which allow the buyer to back out without penalty and without a substantial reason to do so. I have seen clauses like "subject to my accountant's approval". As a buyer, this is nice, as a seller it is not beneficial because there is little to no commitment on the buyer's behalf.

**If you want an iron-clad contract,
then it cannot be subject to anything.**

Sellers want an iron clad contract because they want out. You as a buyer have more complicated motives. You want to avoid as much expense as possible, you want to minimize your risk and you want to be sure you are buying a property free from a myriad of potential problems. It is a game of cat and mouse because the seller usually knows the condition of a property and is not obligated to share any deficiencies or issues they are aware of with you. Then of course there are other issues that may arise that the seller was not even aware of, that your inspections and due diligence may uncover. Sellers sometimes need time to digest new information and adjust their pricing perspective to give a reduction on an already agreed upon price.

Engineers reports, termite inspections and similar requirements are usually addressed between the *acceptance of an offer* by a seller and the signing of a formal *contract of sale*. This allows the buyer to determine if there are any unexpected issues that are a deal breaker or create the need to renegotiate. For this reason, sellers prefer these issues are resolved before entering a contract.

PROFESSIONAL INSPECTIONS

When buying a property, it is a good idea to hire some professionals to protect your interests. Banks require you to do most of these things mentioned here and even if you are not using a bank, this is a prudent course of action. Hiring an appraiser to value the property will tell you a lot about the house and state what the appraiser believes to be the *fair market value*, based on the size, type and quality of construction. The appraiser will also use comparisons of other properties in your area, which will be provided in their report to establish value.

An engineer's report or a similar report from a professional home inspector will provide even more in-depth information about a property than an appraisal or insect inspection. A home inspector will examine the house from the bottom up starting with the foundation, stating if it is in good order and if the general construction of the home is sound. The inspector will work their way up to the roof to verify it is in good condition and free of leaks. Along the way they will ferret out problems or potential problems if they exist, so you may become aware of potential major expenses you would not be anticipating. The inspector will examine crawl spaces, attics, basements, and any other accessible areas to determine if there are any issues to be noted in their report.

All systems, including heating, plumbing, air conditioning, electrical systems, and appliances will be checked. The exterior is also carefully examined. As a result of the detail in this type of report, you will undoubtedly have a checklist of minor things that you may want to attend to, even if all goes well. Knowing there are no major issues can also make the cost of the inspection worthwhile.

DEAL BREAKERS

A *deal breaker* can be defined as the point in a negotiation where one of the parties is willing to allow the deal to fall apart. Most deal breakers occur during the negotiation of a contract, but occasionally they can happen at the closing. Sometimes deal breakers are legal issues and other times they may be personal in nature. Sometimes either party will not be getting what they want from a negotiation and other times it may be that the problem is simply a difference of perspective that is not reconcilable.

After an initial agreement is made, additional previously undisclosed information such as environmental issues that arise could be *cause* to cancel a deal. If an engineer's report discovers the foundation of a house is crumbling and must be replaced it could be a deal breaker for a buyer, even if a seller is willing to repair it.

Sometimes taking a firm stance on a position in a negotiation and letting the other party know the issue is a deal breaker for you will sway them to give in or change their position so you can move ahead, otherwise you should just walk away.

AS IS

"*As Is*" are the two scariest words in the real estate world for a buyer because they work to the seller's advantage in a contract. The use of "as is" condition is common when buying foreclosures and distressed properties. Again, buyer beware is the rule of the day here. These two words can cost you untold thousands of dollars. Do some serious homework before agreeing to this contingency, so you will better understand the risks you are considering.

I accept "as is" language for things like condition of appliances and other things that can be easily replaced, or an inspection will determine if they are in reasonable condition. You should require CO's, a survey, an appraisal, and a home inspection report too.

**Every deal should be subject to clear title
and your attorney can fully explain the risks
associated with various defects in a title.**

CONTRACT

When your offer to purchase a property is accepted by a seller, the next step is to enter into a formal written *contract of sale*.

CHAPTER 8
THE CONTRACT

When a buyer and seller agree on a selling price, it will be formalized with other terms of the deal in a written contract. Contracts spell out certain things that the buyer and seller must do, known as *contractual obligations*, and when they must be done. Some items need to be attended to quickly, while others may be addressed at any time before the deed is transferred. A statement that the contract represents the full or entire agreement between the parties and that no other agreement, written or verbal has been made or may be bound against either party is typically included.

A written agreement is always required so it may be enforceable in a court if either party defaults on their obligations under the agreement. A contract must also include certain things to be deemed valid, such as:

- The legal names of the persons or entities, also known as the *parties* to the transaction for both the buyer and seller.
- The date the transaction is entered into and is expected to be concluded by, known as the *closing date*.

- The physical address of the property but preferably the *legal description* of the property.
- The agreed upon purchase price.
- A *meeting of the minds*, or an agreement to the terms that have been included by all parties to the transaction.
- Signatures of sellers whom are on the deed to be transferred or have the legal right to transfer the deed as well as all buyers whose name the deed is to be transferred to.
- Good and valuable *consideration*, which is what the buyer is tendering to the seller to purchase the property. Consideration can be money, anything a buyer might barter or a promise to pay.
- Who will pay for specific expenses such as closing costs, real estate taxes etc. (real estate taxes are usually prorated).
- Condition of property or sold *"as is"*.

Contracts must also have a legal purpose such as the transfer of real property to be enforceable. Illegal transactions, although seemingly obvious, would be voided and not enforceable in a court.

Buyers and sellers must both have entered into the agreement willingly and neither party may be under *duress*, meaning pressured or forced to sign an agreement. Signers must be of sound mind and not under the influence of narcotics or other substances. Minors may enter into a contract, but they have certain rights to cancel a contract.

Sometimes when an offer is made to purchase a home, not much more than the price or what personal items in a home might be included in the offering price is discussed. After the initial agreement is made, many other considerations or contingencies may begin to arise. This is when a buyer or seller decides to add certain provisions to create a more encompassing understanding of the agreement.

Some of the items to be negotiated are settled upon before the preparation of the written contracts while others will surely arise later. It is not uncommon for a prepared contract to be passed back and forth between parties several times to settle open issues. Everything from the date the transfer will take place to what is or is not included in the agreement may be discussed. Once all the issues are settled upon and both parties are in full agreement, the contracts are ready to be signed.

CONTRACT LANGUAGE

Contracts are typically composed of two segments; one termed *boilerplate language* and the other is a *rider*. The boilerplate language is what you might consider standard clauses which address a myriad of items that usually are acceptable to both parties but can be changed by either party so long as there is agreement to do so. Prepared boilerplate language in the form of *standardized legal forms* save attorneys lots of time in preparing contracts. Because lawyers who do substantial real estate work are familiar with the language within these forms, they can focus on the items which are generally more negotiable and relevant to your transaction that would be added to a contract in the form of a *rider*. When lawyers save time, you save money!

RIDERS

A rider is simply an additional page or pages added to the main body of a contract which becomes part of the contract. This practice is common and almost every real estate contract includes a rider of some sort due to the complexity and unique circumstances of most transactions. Riders address specific needs and contingencies set by the parties and items not otherwise included in the contact.

Because certain language might be duplicated or conflicting in a rider and the main body of a contract, language such as "In the event of a conflict between the terms and provisions of this agreement and the rider, those terms and conditions set forth in the rider shall prevail" is usually added to the rider for clarification purposes.

If your property is subject to rules of a Homeowner's Association (HOA) or any other rules, then those rules may also become part of the contract as a rider. Seller's representations and warranties or required repairs, addressing environmental issues that may arise and items that an agreement may be subject to are more examples of things that may be found in a rider.

SUBJECT TO

Subject to clauses are negotiated terms included in a contract that make a contract subject to cancellation by either party, without penalty. The buyer would be entitled to a full refund of their deposit but not necessarily any expenses they incurred such as paying for a survey unless this was addressed in the contract. Conversely if all the contingencies have been met, a buyer can no longer withdraw from the agreement without penalty.

The classic example would be a clause such as "This agreement is subject to (or *contingent upon*) the buyer obtaining a mortgage in the amount of $100,000.00 at an interest rate not to exceed 4.5%." Most buyers will readily agree to this because it is understood that without the ability to obtain a mortgage, a buyer cannot meet the commitment to finalize the purchase. A time frame to obtain a mortgage and other limitations are typically included and these often-become negotiating points immediately prior to signing of the contracts.

Other common examples of contingencies are "the appraised value must meet or exceed the sales price", "tenants must be removed" or "sale of the buyer's home".

When a contract is subject to a buyer selling their home, it should avoid vague language, because this contingency in its simplicity does not address things such as a time frame for closing, at what price or under what conditions the house is to be sold. A seller would have to weigh the time their property could be off the market for sale against the likelihood the deal will come to fruition. Most sellers want a more definitive deal, yet many will accept this condition if they have confidence in the buyer's ability to complete their transaction in a timely manner. More often this clause is acceptable when a buyer already has a signed contract in hand for the sale of their home and the timing needs to be worked out, so they have the money available to buy the new home.

TERMITE INSPECTIONS
In areas where insects such as termites or other wood destroying insects capable of damaging a house are prevalent, an inspection might uncover major problems that could be a deal breaker; or the

report may state everything is fine and you can take possession with peace of mind.

Termite inspections are usually completed within ten days or so before the contracts are signed. This serves to avoid incurring legal and other expenses if the buyer and seller cannot agree on how to remedy any issues that may be found during these types of inspections.

Generally, if a contract is subject to an inspection, attorneys will not move forward with title searches and other work before the inspection is completed and the house is determined to be free of infestation and damage or steps are taken to remedy any negative findings. This must be satisfactory to both parties, unless liability for repairs is addressed within the contract.

SETTING A CLOSING DATE

Under normal circumstances a buyer and seller will agree to an approximate date upon which money and deed can be exchanged. Because banks may need additional time to process a loan application or a seller isn't ready to move, either side generally has the option to change the agreed upon closing date once without challenge or liability. An extension of only a few days may be needed but thirty days is common. Therefore, the closing date is usually stated in a contract as *on or about*, indicating this is acceptable.

In some instances, such as when houses are sold by banks that have come out of foreclosure or deals do not have contingencies, then the term *on or before* a specified date may be used. As the term implies, the date set is expected to be a hard date that may not be moved back although closing sooner would be acceptable.

As previously noted, when a closing date is established, and the term *time is of the essence* is added by either the buyer or seller this indicates the transaction MUST be completed by the specified dates without any extension. The underlying reason for this would most likely be that one of the parties will suffer damages or irreparable harm such as losing the opportunity to by another property based on this transaction. Another common reason for the insertion of "time is of the essence" clauses has to do with tax consequences.

Failure to meet a "time is of the essence" requirement can carry substantial penalties and additional charges to cover costs incurred by the party which has been harmed. This makes sense because the party in default was aware of the requirement being added to make the deal work for the other party. While these terms establish the legal rights of the parties, please remember any agreement can be modified if both parties are willing to make a change.

POSSESSION DATE

The closing date is usually the day a buyer takes possession, but it does not have to be. A seller may want to stay in the premises after the property has changed hands and will pay the new owner rent for a specified period. Legal transfer of possession is evidenced by the transfer of the deed, while the transfer of the keys when the closing is complete is the traditional symbolic transfer of possession.

It is common practice for the buyer to do a walk through just before the closing to insure the house is ready to be delivered in the condition as agreed and all personal items included in the contract are still present.

The proximity of the house to the place of closing needs to be considered. I usually schedule a walk through two hours before the closing. The seller or a broker will normally be present to provide access to the property.

In the event something has gone awry or a discrepancy arises during the walk-through process, this can then be addressed at the closing by reaching an agreement to remedy the problem. Reductions in money due, money placed in escrow or a simple promise to rectify a situation are normal ways parties resolve most issues.

SIGNED CONTRACTS

Contracts are signed by both parties either at the same time or individually and exchanged via mail or by other means of delivery. Contracts may be signed in counterparts, meaning each party will sign different copies of the same contract which will be exchanged when circumstances require this. Typically, as a buyer, once you have signed the contracts and returned them to the seller with the agreed upon deposit, the seller will countersign them. If attorneys are involved, upon countersigning the seller's attorney will send your attorney a *fully executed* contract with both signatures and you have a legal binding agreement subject to whatever terms are contained within that agreement.

Note that contracts can have any number of signers, such as husband and wife on the sellers' side and a partnership requiring four signatures if the buyer is a partnership of two couples. The names of those on the deed to be sold and the names on the deed to be recorded are typically those who have signed the contract, but not always.

Contract signatures generally do not have to be notarized. Original signatures are required to make a real estate contract enforceable under the law, therefore, electronic signatures are only acceptable if permissible by law in a specific jurisdiction. Real estate contracts are not usually recorded documents like a deed as they are only written agreements and do not represent the outcome of a transaction such as the physical transfer of a deed evidencing transfer of ownership.

Some contracts are transferable, and some are not, the language within the contract as agreed upon by the parties will define this. A transferable contract is just that, a buyer could flip a purchase to another buyer, potentially for a tidy profit if the contract allows for transferability. Obviously, many sellers want a binding contract with the buyer, so it is commonplace for lawyers to include non-transferable language in a contract.

CORPORATE OWNERSHIP

Can you buy a house in a company name or is there another form of ownership? Yes, but most first-time home buyers are going to live in the home and take title in their own names. Any legal entity can own real estate and depending on the purpose of the entity, when allowable by law, a Corporation, Limited Liability Corporation, Partnership, Trust etc., can own property. Generally, for tax and liability purposes too complex to discuss here, an LLC is the preferred way to take ownership of a property if you are not purchasing the property in your own name.

If you are going to purchase a property in the name of an entity instead of your name and have not formed that entity yet, your lawyer can add language to a contract giving you the right to do so before closing on the property. You can sign contracts in your personal name and at closing, put the deed into a company name. As an investor, I have done this often, yet my own home is in my name. As a buyer, you might be purchasing a property from another form of legal entity if it was owned by a bank, an investor or a realtor.

By creating a legal entity such as an LLC (Limited Liability Company) you essentially change or transfer the ownership of a property from your name into a company name. This serves as a layer of legal defense to protect your other personal assets from any potential lawsuits where you might otherwise become personally liable. In the simplest sense, if someone slips and falls on your property, they would sue the company instead of you personally. Only the value of the assets in the company would be at risk, not your other personal assets. Since a home is usually the largest asset a first-time home buyer will own, and the home is insured with liability coverage, forming an entity for protection of other assets is not usually necessary. If you have significant assets, this might be worth discussing with your attorney.

UUMBRELLA INSURANCE

You can also protect yourself by carrying a large *umbrella insurance policy*. An umbrella policy is like an add on to your basic property insurance which only becomes activated if a claim in excess of your regular insurance policy limit should occur. Umbrella insurance is relatively cheap since the value of the underlying policy acts as a deductible before the umbrella policy would have to pay out any settlement. Your insurance agent can guide towards selecting a policy that is right for you.

TITLE

Now your lawyer will order a *title search* to confirm you are buying what you think you are. Attorneys use a *title company* to accomplish this. The title company will research the history, chain of ownership and previous transfers of a property to detect potential problems with the title. Your attorney will receive a *title report* from the title company which should verify that you are receiving a *clear title* to the property you are purchasing. This means there are no liens, also stated in legal terms as *free of liens, defects or encumbrances* upon the property which could reduce its value, limit your use in some way or create potential litigation problems for you down the road.

Sometimes a title report will show one or more *defects* or problems with the title to the parcel of property which you have contracted to purchase. You may accept a title with a defect or allow time for the seller to *cure* or fix the defect. If the problem cannot be resolved, you may have to agree to accept the title "as is" with the defect. This is a business decision that you will discuss with your attorney or other professionals if the need arises. Need I say hire an experienced *real estate attorney*? The title company will then issue a *Title Insurance Policy*, with or without *exclusions of liability* based on their findings.

When the attorneys have completed their work and the bank has approved your loan, a *closing date* will be scheduled. At this point, now that you are familiar with some of what you can expect when reading a contract, it is time to hire a lawyer to have your own contract prepared.

LAWYERS

The time to hire a lawyer is BEFORE you sign a contract. Hire a lawyer with real estate experience, not every lawyer is an expert in every area of law. Check what the requirements are in your state, as some states do not require an attorney to transfer real property and some do. Even if you are not required to use an attorney, I would advise you to retain one to represent you because the cost of an error or omission could be much more than the attorney's fee. States such as Florida require only one attorney who can represent both parties in a transaction.

In two attorney states, like New York, where the buyer and seller are each represented by their own attorney, both parties will hire a lawyer. The seller's attorney will usually draw up the contracts and submit them to the buyer's attorney for review and proposed changes, but the buyer's attorney could draft the contracts if the seller is willing to allow this.

When the buyer's attorney receives the contracts, some questions are likely to arise. Your attorney might see a liability you could incur and recommend you act to resolve the point before moving forward. Often there are additional changes to the language in a contract that your attorney will request or insist upon before allowing you to sign the documents. Sometimes the seller or the seller's attorney has added some language that was not agreed upon or discussed.

As you might imagine, two lawyers negotiating a contract on behalf of their clients can create more adversarial situations than two clients using a common lawyer where agreement may be reached more easily. Lawyers are supposed to provide legal advice and you are supposed to make the business decisions, but sometimes the lines get blurred in a negotiation when two attorneys butt heads. In the end, it is you who should set the terms of the business deal, tempered by the advice of the professional you have hired to represent you.

On more than one occasion, I have had to step in between lawyers and/or real estate brokers to renegotiate or clarify agreements with a seller to keep a deal together. Lawyers have also prevented me from making some potentially costly mistakes. You need to be proactive, stay informed and speak up if things are not going as you think they should. Sometimes a sticking point can create a divide.

How you bridge the gap and attempt to settle differences with a seller will determine whether your deal will move forward or not. It is okay to concede on some points, but never give in just to make a deal. If you do not like the terms, you can withdraw from a negotiation at any time BEFORE you sign a contract of sale, without legal or financial obligation to the seller.

POWER OF ATTORNEY
In some instances, a buyer or seller, also known as a *principal* in a real estate transaction, may exercise a right to use a *power of attorney*, which

allows their lawyer to sign documents on their behalf. Attorneys can represent their clients with *full powers* allowing them to make all decisions relating to their client or with *specific powers*, such as the ability to purchase a property on behalf of their client, either of which would be outlined in the power of attorney agreement.

CHAPTER 9
HOW IS YOUR CREDIT SCORE?

If you are thinking of buying a home, even before you start shopping, it is a good idea to learn what your *credit score,* also known as a *FICO score,* is. Lenders will rely on your credit score and a *credit report* they receive from a *credit bureau* to determine what they believe is your creditworthiness and ability to repay the money you are asking to borrow.

The higher your credit score is, the more likely you are to be successful when applying for credit of any kind. FICO scores range between 300 and 850. Credit rankings can be summarized as follows:

> Under 630....................Poor
> 630 - 690......................Fair
> 690 - 720....................Good
> Above 720...........Excellent

The three most commonly used credit agencies are Equifax, Trans Union and Experian. Although all three companies track similar information, each calculates its own score, therefore you will have three scores that may potentially be used by any lender, even though many lenders may only work with one. For this reason, you will want to check your report with all three companies to verify the accuracy of each one.

A great credit score may also allow you to get a preferred interest rate and other perks from credit card companies. Conversely, a low credit score can hurt your chances of being approved or result in an approval but at a higher interest rate which could cost you more money over time.

Banks rely on credit reporting agencies or credit bureaus to check your credit. They receive a copy of your credit report for a fee. In addition to a score, the report shows the current state of your outstanding credit along with your credit and payment history. You are entitled to a free annual credit report from each of the bureaus because of amendments made to *The Fair Credit Reporting Act*, so you may review the content of your reports.

You may be able to improve your score and should certainly make every effort possible to fix any negative, missing or incorrect data before a potential lender investigates your financial background.

Also check that all debts you have paid off are noted as such on your credit report. There are companies that will help you reduce or eliminate bad marks on a credit report and increase your score for a fee, if your credit is seriously in need of repair. The primary things that affect your credit score in weighted order are:

- Do you make timely payments on open balances as agreed?

- How much money do you currently owe to others?

- How long is your credit history?

- What type of credit do you have? Such as a Mortgage (Secured) vs Credit Card (Unsecured) debt.

- Have you had a lot of recent inquiries? (Too many can lower your score)

- Outstanding debt ratio to credit available.

- Length of employment and employment history

Many things can affect your credit score and it is important to note that sometimes a lot of available credit, which is not the same as outstanding credit, can hurt you as well. While it sounds counter intuitive, banks are always concerned that you might max out all the credit available to you after they make a loan. Banks will factor into the equation what your maximum debt could be and not what it is. Therefore, this may be the time to consider closing dormant credit card accounts that you have no intention of using or have not used for a long time.

How you pay your rent and utility bills is not tracked by credit reporting agencies, so they will not affect your credit score unless you become delinquent and are reported as such.

Credit agencies also track negative information found in public records relating to your credit worthiness. Your credit history would include any type of recorded debt such as credit cards, loans, liens, bankruptcies and other financing you may have applied for. The balances you carry, and the timeliness of your payments are tracked as well.

Examples of big negatives that will hurt your credit score for a long time are a *chapter 7 bankruptcy* within the last ten years or a *chapter 13 bankruptcy* within the last seven years. An eviction, a foreclosure or extremely late unpaid obligations will also result in lower credit scores and take some effort to repair.

Many credit inquiries from potential lenders over time, known as *credit shopping* in the lending industry, can lower your credit score. The good news is, multiple inquires related to a similar loan such as a mortgage or a car loan made within a 45-day window are usually considered as a single event. You may also notice recent inquiries do not appear on your report because of a lag time in reporting and recording this information.

You should also know that lenders may check your credit scores during the pre-approval stage and may re-check them again just before closing a loan to be sure your credit status has not changed significantly since they agreed to your pre-approval and they hand over the money.

GET PRE-QUALIFIED

The *pre-qualification* process works well when you have a relationship with a bank or can select a bank that you want to borrow from before you start shopping for a home. You can submit a loan application for review and a bank will tell you how much they would be willing to lend to you based on your credit and income. A letter of pre-qualification tells sellers you are a serious buyer and lets them know the approval process for a final mortgage commitment should go smoothly for a loan up to the amount designated in the approval letter the bank will give you.

Pre-approval is very helpful if you run into a seller that is pressured to close on a property or has lost one or more buyers who made offers but could not get their financing approved. This costs sellers time and potentially money so pre-qualification will appeal to many sellers.

Pre-qualification also removes a lot of the anxiety new home buyers face, hoping to get the house they want. It allows you to work within a budget, knowing your limits and gives you the ability to make a more intelligent offer. Sometimes pre-approval can even aid you in negotiating a better deal. If a seller knows the maximum loan you are approved for is less than their asking price, they will have to decide if they want to close the gap in price to make a deal or let you buy someone else's house.

WHAT IF YOU ARE NOT APPROVED?

If you are denied credit because of information contained in your credit report, then your lender is required to send you a *denial letter* which must state the reason for denial of your application. Your lender is also required to provide you with instructions about how to obtain this free copy of your credit report. As per The Fair Credit Reporting Act receipt of a denial letter entitles you to request a free copy of your credit report, in addition to the free annual report you are entitled to.

You must request a report based on a denial letter within 60 days, which can be done online.

Here are the web sites for the top three credit bureaus.

https://www.experian.com/
https://www.transunion.com/
https://www.equifax.com/personal/

If a review of your credit report shows that it contains errors, you may dispute the errors to have them removed. If your credit score improves because of resolved disputes you could reapply for the loan that was denied. You should know that credit bureaus only report information they collect, or which is submitted to them, they do not make credit decisions.

CHAPTER 10
THE LANGUAGE OF LOANS

Understanding the nomenclature used within the world of lending will make it easier to shop for a mortgage and absorb the content of agreements you will be signing. Here is some of the basic terminology you will come across:

TERM

How long will you want to borrow the money for? The length of the loan is called the *term* by bankers. The most traditional terms are 30 years or 15 years, but longer and shorter terms are available.

LTV

Loan to Value Ratio or LTV is used by lenders to calculate the maximum size of a loan they are willing to make in relation to the value of the property. The ratio is stated in the form of a percentage such as 80% LTV. In this case on a $100,000 house the maximum loan a bank would approve will be $80,000. Therefore, the minimum down payment required would be 20%. On a 70% LTV loan you would have to put down a minimum of 30% to be approved and so forth.

INTEREST RATE

For a *fixed rate loan*, the bank will tell you what the interest rate is. For a *variable rate loan*, the bank uses a published *index* or barometer which it ties to the rate they will charge you. A bank can use any index it discloses to the borrower, however most banks underwriting adjustable rate loans currently use one of the first three indexes:

CMT   (Constant Maturity Treasury)

COFI   (Cost of Funds Index - 11th District)

LIBOR (London Interbank Offered Rate)

Other examples of indexes are:

The Prime Rate

Federal Funds Rate

12 Month Treasury Average

10 Year Treasury Security or T-Bills

(Treasury Securities)

Certificate of Deposit Index

Discount Rate

Fannie Mae 30/60

LIBOR is a wholesale variable interest rate at which banks will lend money to each other. A *margin*, which is the banks profit and does not vary over the life of a loan, is added to the LIBOR rate to calculate what the bank will charge you.

If the loan language calls for an interest rate of LIBOR plus 2%, you can monitor the LIBOR rate which is published daily and add two percent to arrive at your actual rate. So, you are asking yourself if your loan rate will adjust daily? The short answer is probably not. Variable rates usually adjust as explained below under the heading *Adjustable Rate Mortgages*.

APR

Annual Percentage Rate or APR is the calculation of what you will pay on an annual basis because of compounding. The published APR of a loan is usually lower than the interest rate for loans with regular monthly payments. Because a loan's balance reduces with each payment, the total interest paid, and the APR become slightly lower than the annual interest rate.

CAPS

To protect the consumer from steep increases in interest rates lenders may offer CAPS or limits on the amount the interest rate may increase in any adjustment period. These are known as *Adjustment Caps*. Two percent per year is what I have typically seen for annual adjustment caps. In addition, loans may have *Lifetime Caps*. While the spread between the interest rate you will be paying and the lifetime cap the lender is offering may sound like a lot when you agree to this type of loan, if you reach the cap it would mean market rates have really risen more than you expected. In this case, if you had a crystal ball, you would have opted for a fixed rate loan from the start.

Lenders created the concept of caps on interest rates because they realized borrowers would not want to take loans with the open-ended liability of rising interest rates. Loans without rate caps could subject you to much higher interest rates than you would expect, as was the case when rates reached just over 18.5% per annum in the height of the mortgage madness during 1981. The gap between your interest rate and the cap of a loan also allows lenders the opportunity to make a larger return or profit on a loan in a rising interest rate environment.

RATE LOCKS
When shopping for a loan, interest rates may be rising or falling. If rates are falling, procrastinating or taking your time to sign on the dotted line may save you some money, but if rates are rising, it could cost you more money daily. Banks offer you an option you can take advantage of when there is a degree of uncertainty in interest rates called a *rate lock*. A rate lock is usually given for a period, such as thirty to sixty days from pre-approval until closing but other options exist.

If a loan is not made within the rate lock period, the interest rate may revert to whatever the current market rates are.

Banks charge a fee for rate locks that is typically built into the interest rate they will quote you. You should expect to pay an additional fee if you request an extension of time if you haven't finalized the loan before your rate lock expires.

Timing when you lock in a rate is important. You wouldn't want to lock in a rate after pre-approval if you didn't have a signed purchase contract yet. If you do it too early in the process the deadline may expire leaving you looking at market rates again. Likewise, you wouldn't want to pay a higher fee for a long-term rate lock if you expect to close on a property within the next 45 days. Also know that under some circumstances lenders may be able to reject a rate lock if you fail to meet some of the criteria in the fine print.

BUY DOWNS

Banks will also let you reduce or *buy down* the interest rate on a loan by paying a premium up front. The premium, which is prepaid interest from an accounting perspective, is called a point. A point is the equivalent of 1% of the amount of money you borrow. What this means in dollars is one point on a $100,000 loan would be $1,000. Banks will set the amount you can reduce the interest rate by per point or fraction of a point paid and the maximum number of points you can buy. Banks commonly allow you to pay up to four points, but you may elect not to pay any.

As an example, you may be able to reduce the interest rate of your loan by ¼ of 1% per point you pay. I know this doesn't sound like much but paying $1,000 up front to save a quarter of a percent on a $100,000 loan would result in a savings of $250 per year ($100,000 x .0025 = $250). The savings will be reduced as the loan balance is paid down. On a thirty-year loan the total savings for a half point reduction in interest rate from 5% to 4.5% would be about $10,850 per $100,000 borrowed.

All points are not created equally. One lender might reduce your interest rate by 0.125% per point while another might reduce it by .25%. Even though these numbers look small and seem similar at first glance, don't be fooled! There is a 100% difference between these numbers when you absorb the math. Using the 0.125% number you would need to pay 8 points to reduce the interest rate on a loan by 1% and in the second example of .25% you would only need to purchase 4 points to achieve the same 1% interest rate reduction. Remember, while the value of the buy down can change, a point is a constant calculation pegged at 1% of the loan value.

Compare these two scenarios for a 30-year loan:

Bank 1 is offering a $100,000 loan
at a 3.75% interest rate

Bank 2 is offering a $100,000 loan
at a 4.00% interest rate

At face value, it is obvious that Bank 1 is offering a better interest rate and you will pay a lot less interest over time with their loan and that would be true. But let's say both banks will allow you to buy down their loans through the purchasing of points. Each point at 1% will cost you $1,000 at either bank.

Bank 1 is offering a .0125% reduction per point
Bank 2 is offering a .25% reduction per point
Both banks have a limit of four points that can be purchased.

This means each bank is allowing you to pay up to $4,000 (4 points x $1,000 each) to reduce your interest rate. Here is the impact of the difference in the cost of the points:

Bank 1
3.75% initial rate 30-year, $100,000 loan
Regular monthly payment $463

Total interest for life of the loan would be $66,722
3.5% rate after points, 4 points x .0125% reduction
New monthly payment $449
A savings of $14 per month
Total interest for life of the loan would be $61,656

It would take 285 months (23 years) to break even after paying $4,000 in points. Your total savings would only be $1,066 over 30 years ($66,722 - $61,656 less $4,00 points = $1,066). And, your interest paid would be $61,656 plus $4,000 in points for a total of $65,656.

Bank 2
4% initial rate 30-year, $100,000 loan
Regular monthly payment $477
Total interest for life of the loan would be $71,870
3.0% rate after points (4 points x .25% reduction)
New monthly payment $422
A savings of $55 per month
Total interest for life of the loan would be $51,777

It would only take about 72 months (6 years) to break even after paying $4,000 in points when borrowing from Bank 2. Your total savings would now be $16,093 over 30 years ($71,870 - $51,777 less $4,00 points = $16,093). And, your interest paid would be $51,777 plus $4,000 in points for a total of $55,777.

As you can see, the lower rate initially offered by Bank 1 costs more money than the higher initial rate offered by Bank 2 over the life of the loan. This is solely the result of the interest rate adjustment from buying points. The net difference in these two offerings could save you or cost you a grand total of **$9,879** depending on which loan you choose and that's on a small interest rate difference. The savings in these examples multiplies as the amount of money borrowed increases. Using the multiplier, you can visualize the significant savings that could be achieved when shopping for a $250,000 loan.

**I know this is a lot of math,
but the savings can truly be astonishing!**

Sometimes banks like to talk in fractions for some numbers and percentages for others, which makes it a little more difficult for some consumers to differentiate between the costs of loans offered. Three eights of a percent are simply calculated as three divided by 8 or .375%. If you always convert fractions to decimals you will be able to compare apples to apples more easily.

How do you know if it pays to buy one or more points? You simply take the amount it will cost you per point and divide that by the number of months or mortgage payments the savings will take to pay for the buy down. Here is the math without adjusting for compounding or reduced balances:

$100,000 Loan at
5.00% = $5,000 per year in interest

$100,000 Loan (After paying points) at
4.75% = $4,750 per year in interest

Savings = $250 per year ($5,000 - $4,750)

A cost of $1,000 to buy down the rate divided by
$250 = 4 years to break even.

You would then enjoy the value of the reduced interest rate over the life of the loan. Therefore, the longer the term of your loan is, the more advantageous it is to buy down the rate. The simple mathematical calculation above will allow you to compute the break-even point and compare different buy down rates based on interest rate reduction and cost of the points.

The key to figuring out how much to buy down a loan lies in how much of a discount on the interest rate a bank is willing to give you per point and how many points they will let you buy.

You might be asking yourself if there is a downside to buying points and yes there are two potential negatives. The first being, after adding up all the expenses of buying a new home, will you have the extra cash available to buy the points? A $200,000 loan with four points at $2,000 per point would be $8,000 more cash needed to acquire your mortgage. The silver lining here is you will have another $8,000 tax deduction and if you are in the top tax bracket our Uncle Sam will pick up as much as half the tab when you file your tax return.

The second negative comes into play if you are not planning to live in the property beyond where the interest break-even point is, or you sell before that point in time for some unexpected reason. In either of these cases, don't forget to factor in the after-tax results of the upfront cost of the points you paid.

ORIGINATION FEE

A loan is *originated* when a borrower applies, and the term *origination* also includes the complete process of approving or declining a loan. Most lenders charge an *origination fee*, also expressed as a point or a fraction of a point when originating a loan. This is another form of reimbursement or profit for the bank with a fancy name. When a loan is not started with the bank that ends up servicing the loan, the originator of the loan would keep this fee as part of their compensation or as a commission when reselling the loan.

Origination fees are one area where you can negotiate with a bank if you are making a larger loan. It costs a bank almost the same money to underwrite a loan for $100,000 as it does for a loan of $500,000. Therefore, the fee of one point on the $100,000 loan of $1,000 compared to $5,000 for the $500,000 loan is disproportionate in terms of profitability. This leaves the bank enough room to negotiate and still make a large profit for their effort.

PRE-PAYMENT PENALTIES

Most traditional mortgages do not have prepayment penalties, as the banks have already built their fee structure to collect much of their costs up front. However, loan products that offer low initial rates or teaser rates may come with a pre-payment penalty. A pre-payment penalty is a way for a lender to recoup costs or some of the potential lost profit by letting you out of a deal earlier than they anticipated.

Unless you have come across a great loan offer and have no reasonable expectation of paying your loan off early, try to avoid taking a loan with a pre-payment penalty whenever possible. You never know what the future holds, and you may want to pay the loan off sooner than you thought.

TAXES

Home mortgage interest, origination fees and any other prepaid interest such as points are tax deductible. Fees charged by lenders for underwriting a loan are not tax deductible. For these reasons, having a copy of your closing statement handy around tax filing time will be appreciated by your accountant who will use this to write off the appropriate expenses for you.

CHAPTER 11
TYPES OF MORTGAGES

Although the lending process can be cumbersome, banks try to keep things simple for the consumer, to make it easier to sign you up. One of the first things you will want to know is the type of loan you are looking for. Most first-time home buyers will be looking for an *owner occupied*, traditional *first mortgage* simply referred to in the generic sense as a *mortgage*. These four categories of loans are what most consumers see advertised and know about:

30-year fixed rate
30-year adjustable rate
15-year fixed rate
15-year adjustable rate

There are two broad categories of mortgage loans, which are conforming and non-conforming loans. A conforming loan or conventional mortgage must meet the guidelines and limits set by the *Federal Housing Finance Agency* (FHFA). Loans that qualify under FHFA rules may be purchased or guaranteed by *Fannie Mae* or *Freddie Mac*, which will mean little to you as the borrower but allows the lender to resell your loan very easily.

FHA LOANS

Not to be confused with the FHFA just mentioned, the FHA or *Federal Housing Administration* lends money with as little as a 3.5% down payment if you have a credit score of 580 or more. If your credit score is lower, but you put more money down, you may still qualify for an FHA loan. Many first-time home buyers will use this program to purchase a home because of the lower down payment requirements. Mortgage insurance is required, so this will be an additional initial cost, but this requirement can be waived when you accumulate more substantial equity in the property. FHA loans are only offered by banks that have been approved by the FHA.

CONVENTIONAL FIXED RATE MORTGAGES

A 30-year Conventional Fixed Rate Mortgage is a mortgage most people are familiar with. It's composed of a fixed rated for a fixed period. Equal monthly payments are made for the duration of the loan, which will be paid off in thirty years. While this loan suits most home buyer's needs, you may want to consider some other options.

If you are planning to move in a few years a thirty-year loan may not be the best option for you. This is because you will have accumulated very little equity from your payments which have been composed of almost entirely interest, taxes and insurance, not principal. You might consider a shorter term to pay less interest, which for conventional fixed rate loans is typically 20, 15 or 10 years.

The two primary advantages of a shorter-term loan are you can usually get a lower interest rate and you will pay off the principal much faster. This allows you to build equity while reducing the total interest paid on a loan. In chapter 13 titled *Calculating Loan Costs*, I have added tables comparing 15-year and 30-year payment schedules with remaining balance figures.

ADJUSTABLE RATE MORTGAGES

Adjustable rate mortgages or *ARM's* are loans on which the interest rates can adjust upward or downward depending on current market rates at the time an adjustment is scheduled. Adjustable rate mortgages usually have multiple adjustment periods. By spacing these periods of change in the interest rate, consumers don't have to focus on what the market interest rates are doing daily.

Lenders tie adjustable rate mortgages to *indexes* that are published regularly and provide an unbiased representation of the interest rate market to be fair to the lender and borrower. Remember there are thousands of mortgages written daily so there needs to be a benchmark to work from. This benchmark is used to determine the rate the lender will charge you.

A lender will add, or in rare instances subtract, a factor or margin from the index to establish the rate they will charge you. As an example, if the index used is LIBOR, then your interest rate will be stated as something to the effect of LIBOR +2%. Obviously, if your loan rate is going to be pegged to an index, you should take a moment to research the index to understand how it may react to changes in the interest rate market over time.

Adjustable rate loans typically have an *anniversary date* also called the *adjustment date* upon which the rate is adjusted to the then current published rate for the index described in the loan documents. A loan can have an adjustment date every year or on the fifth anniversary, every 10th anniversary etc.

HYBRID MORTGAGES

Hybrid loans use a combination of fixed rates and adjustable rates. These loans appeal to borrowers because they have the benefit of a fixed rate for an initial term, such as five or seven years and then the loan converts to an adjustable interest rate. If you feel interest rates will be going down in the next few years this could be a good bet that could lower your carrying costs.

Another advantage of a hybrid loan is that they can buy some time for new homeowners to make renovations or rebuild their savings for a while before rates go up, the assumption being they will have stronger buying power as they earn more in the future. In a banker's terms, a 7/1 ARM would be fixed for seven years and then adjust every year after that for the remaining life of the loan. You might also come across a hybrid loan that has an adjustable interest rate for one or more years and then converts to a fixed rate loan for the remainder of the term. This type of loan may also be called a *convertible loan.*

JUMBO LOANS

When you need to borrow more than the limits banks have set for conforming loans, you may need to apply for a *jumbo loan.* The conforming loan limit set by the Federal Housing Finance Agency in 2018 was $453,100 for one-unit properties. A loan more than $453,100 would be a jumbo loan and be considered a non-conforming loan. These loans are handled differently by banks and may require higher credit scores than conforming loans do, with a more detailed credit check. Depending on the housing market you are shopping in, $453,100 may be a very large number or relatively small in comparison to local housing prices.

The loan to value ratio may also need to be lower on a jumbo loan than a conventional mortgage, meaning instead of an 80% loan value against a 20% down payment, you may need to increase your down payment to make the LTV ratio 70% or less. Mathematically this means you would be putting down 30% or more. Banks like you to have more equity at stake when lending larger sums.

BALLOON PAYMENT LOANS

Loans in which the principal and interest are amortized and paid as if the loan were to be paid off over a long period such as thirty years, but then the entire balance must be paid off in a lump sum, in say five years, are called balloon loans. The final payment due is referred to as the *balloon payment*. This type of loan is commonly used by investors who intend to sell or buyers who may have money becoming available soon but don't want to be have the extremely high monthly payments associated with a short-term loan.

INTEREST ONLY LOANS

Interest only loans, as the name implies, require no regular principal payment to the loan so the loan balance remains the same. Principal payments may be called for in increments or as a single lump sum payment at the end of the term. Interest only payments allow borrowers to take advantage of tax deductions, reduce cash flow requirements and improve leverage on their investment. The amount of a monthly mortgage payment with interest only may still be a substantial figure when you factor in the real estate taxes and insurance that would still have to be paid.

CONSTRUCTION LOANS

If your new home is going to be built from the ground up, you would be looking for a *construction loan*. This may also be used if your new home needs a lot of renovation or may be vacant for some time while work is being done. A construction loan could include the cost of the house plus anticipated remodeling costs. Sometimes the proceeds of a construction loan are released in increments, i.e.; a portion of the initial deposit with a contractor may be paid followed by another payment when the foundation is complete, then when framing is complete etc.

BRIDGE LOANS

Although a *bridge loan* is rarely used by first time home buyers, it is a type of loan you should be aware of. A bridge loan is commonly used when you are trying to buy a home while waiting for the proceeds of another home to become available. This loan allows you to buy the new home without having to sell the original home first.

You might find yourself seeking a bridge loan from someone to buy a home if your capital is tied up for other reasons as well. A bridge loan may only be needed for a matter of days, weeks or a few months. The term bridge loan is born of the concept of needing to bridge the gap between when you need the money to purchase a property and when you will have the money. A bridge loan may also be converted to a mortgage when properly recorded.

There is a down side to bridge loans, aside from the cost of carrying two mortgages at the same time for a short time. If something goes awry relating to the source of the funds, such as the deal on the sale of the first house falls through or the money you were expecting is delayed or may no longer be coming in, then you will be bearing the cost of both loans for an indefinite amount of time until you figure out a solution for your dilemma.

100% FINANCING

There are some federal programs for qualified applicants that will finance the full purchase price of a home. The US Department of Agriculture and The US Department of Veterans Affairs offer these. The USDA loans are made in rural areas to families with low or modest income while VA loans are available to veterans and their families.

WRAP AROUND MORTGAGE

A *wrap around mortgage, wrap,* or *piggy-back loan* is a type of loan that is a second mortgage. This loan "wraps" around the first mortgage allowing the seller to help a prospective buyer finance the sale of their property. This can be helpful when the buyer needs more money than a bank is willing to loan, or the rates may be more favorable to borrow some of the money needed from a seller and some from a bank. Banks tend to frown upon piggy back loans and second mortgages because it reduces the equity in a property they have a security interest in.

HOME EQUITY LOANS

While a *home equity loan* will not help you purchase your first home, it may be useful when you qualify for this type of loan to make improvements that you can't afford to do at the time of purchase. Many first-time home buyers purchase a smaller house they can grow into over the coming years as their income and asset base increases. Adding an extension or a dormer to expand living space by using a home equity loan, rather than move to upsize, can be a consideration when selecting your first home.

There are two traditional ways to borrow money using the equity in your home as collateral. Because your property is being used to *secure* these loans, the interest rates are much better than other types of *non-secured* personal loans.

A *home equity line of credit* or *HELOC*, is a line of credit with a revolving credit line that works like a credit card does. You can borrow money against your credit line in small or large increments as often as you want, if you pay the minimum required payments with interest each month. As you repay the principal you have borrowed, your open balance is reduced, and the money becomes available again for your future use. The incredible change in your financial situation this type of loan can provide for you is explained in chapter eleven.

A home equity loan would be an example of a loan that is like a car loan, where you make fixed payments which reduce your balance owed. However, in the case of this type of home equity loan, the principal you repay does not become available for your use again.

Both types of loans would be a second mortgage, if secured by the property. Therefore, they would be *subordinate* to a first mortgage. If recorded, the second mortgage would be recorded *behind* a first mortgage. A home equity loan could also be in a first position if the home was owned free and clear when it was borrowed or if the first mortgage was paid off during the term of the equity loan.

Banks use different formulas to calculate how much they will lend to you in the form of a home equity loan or line of credit, but the same basic ingredients exist in every formula. A bank will consider your credit score or history, your ability to repay the amount you borrow, and the amount of the *net equity* in your home. Net equity is the value of your home less any outstanding loans. Net equity is based on the current appraised value of a property, not the price paid.

As an example, if a home is appraised for $150,000 and there is a first mortgage of $75,000, there would be a net equity of $75,000. If a bank uses a formula of lending 80% *loan to value* or *LTV*, then they would lend up to 80% of the $150,000 or $120,000 less the outstanding debt. This would equal a maximum credit line for a home equity line of $45,000. ($120,000-$75,000 = $45,000)

CHAPTER 12
WORKING WITH A BANK

Banks are the primary source of funds for most people who purchase a home with a traditional down payment and borrow the rest in the form of a mortgage. If you will be borrowing money, you should begin by talking to some bankers. Bankers will welcome the opportunity to speak with you. Relax, this doesn't mean the *Wall Street* types, you just need to visit a few local banks. The idea is to determine what types of loans they make, how long they take to process a typical application and what they will require of you to lend you money.

As much as you may hope that a bank will lend you money to buy a home, the bank is probably equally hopeful that they can lend you the money. Banks don't make money by holding depositor's money, they make money by lending it. Therefore, banks are usually looking for opportunities to lend. How banks define an opportunity is one of the things that makes them different from each other.

The bridge that lies between connecting you with a bank is the credit approval process. This process becomes much easier when you understand what will be required, so you should be as prepared as possible before starting the application process.

Just like you have shopped for the right house to purchase, you must spend some time seeking the right bank to work with. A bank spends a lot of money marketing to potential borrowers and shops for the right people to lend their money to. So, who are these people they are looking for?

You can have good credit or bad credit, lots of assets or no assets, but the bank must be able to see that you can repay the loan you are seeking. When a banker makes a loan, they know the quality of the loan is only as good as the person or collateral that guarantees the loan. Therefore, financially responsible people are the bank's target audience.

DOWN PAYMENT

As noted earlier there are programs offered by the FHA and the USDA that have little to no down payment requirements. However, most home buyers will typically be expected to make a down payment which is a minimum of twenty percent of the purchase price when applying for a traditional mortgage.

While you may not have to put more than the minimum down payment requested to qualify for a loan, making a larger down payment will make your application "healthier" because it reduces the risk the bank must take when lending. You will also enjoy a lower mortgage payment and save on interest expense as well.

YOUR INCOME

When looking at your application to determine if you could repay a loan, banks will only use about thirty percent of your income for purposes of calculating what you can afford for your housing costs. Simply stated, if you make $100,000 a year then only $30,000 or $2,500 per month would be the basis they would use to determine if you could afford the monthly payment associated with the loan you are asking for. While lenders do look at other facets of your financial situation such as assets and credit history, lenders rely heavily on this income formula. Even though accounting for only 30% of your income may sound unreasonable, remember the bank wants to err on the side of caution whenever possible.

NO INCOME CHECK LOANS

In addition to the income formula, banks discount other sources of income such as rental income because of the potential for it to be reduced or lost over the course of the loan. This never made total sense to me because a borrower could just as easily lose their job or other primary source of income over the life of a loan. For borrowers that know they can pay but cannot meet the banks income formula test, there is an option called a no income check loan. These loans have different approval criteria and are not offered by all lenders, but they streamline the process for some borrowers.

OWNER vs NON-OWNER-OCCUPIED
Bankers will ask you if you are going to live in the house you are purchasing. This is because owner *occupied*, and *non-owner-occupied* loans have different lending criteria associated with them. Investors represent a large portion of the buyers in the residential real estate market, but they will be renting or flipping the house. A bank may not want to go through the process of underwriting a long-term loan only to have the house sold in a few months because this will not allow them to recoup some costs and make the profits they anticipated.

Banks have different programs tailored to investor's needs, because investors often borrow in business and corporate names and will not live in the house. Investors usually have a different level of commitment to a bank than a home owner. For example, if the going gets tough an investor might walk away from a house and the loan more readily if the carrying costs become unpalatable whereas a homeowner might do whatever is within their power to keep their home. Larger down payments usually make banks more comfortable lending to investors.

A mortgage is nothing more than a document or set of documents that evidences a debt secured by a piece of real estate and a promise to pay, backed by the full faith and credit of the borrower. Most mortgage payments made by homeowners are comprised of four things; Principal, Interest, Taxes and Insurance known to professionals in the real estate industry by the acronym PITI.

Generally, there are overarching requirements a bank has, and then specific requirements defined by the type of loan you are considering. Imagine if you went into the local office of a large national bank with hundreds or thousands of offices across the country, maybe even around the globe. This might describe the bank you do business with now. You are sitting at the desk with one of over ten thousand employees and you ask to borrow money to buy a house. How much decision-making responsibility do you think this individual could have in a large organization?

So how does a bank lend money? To standardize and streamline the lending process, banks create and offer what they call products. Each product has rules and criteria that must be met for you to qualify to apply for the product. Understanding your needs and the differences in the loan products being offered by banks will help you make an informed decision. For example, one loan product might require a minimum of 20% down payment whereas another might require a 30% down payment. Each of these products could have different interest rates, terms etc. Bankers will offer or sell these products and suggest various products that may be right for you based on the information you provide them with.

I did describe the banker as a salesman, and even though they might not think of themselves or want you to think of them in this regard, they are nonetheless going to try to sell you their brand and their products. While there is nothing wrong with this, please know that not everyone will always be interested in what is best for you, especially if a bank is pushing a promotion with incentives to sign you up at the time you visit a branch. If you feel a lender is not meeting your needs, try another bank.

When you start to consider the multitude of options available it is important to understand the cost and effect each of these may have on the amount of money you will have to pay up front and in total. It is equally important to know that the costs of loans are very different from one another and you may save or spend tens of thousands of dollars over the life of the loan based on the type of loan you ultimately choose.

UNDERWRITING

The person who works with you during the application process is usually a loan officer. A loan officer is the liaison between the back office of a bank and the customer. An underwriter is the person in the back office who verifies your information and makes credit decisions based on the risks perceived by the lender. Borrowers seldom speak directly with underwriters.

The underwriter must determine if you *have the ability* to repay the loan based on your financial circumstances. Having strong credit or significant assets will help you in the underwriting process. If your application does not pass muster in the underwriting process for some reason, it will be sent back to the loan officer who will work with you to submit additional information or correct items, so your application can be resubmitted.

Bear in mind that applicants often have unique circumstances to consider so you may have several requests to provide missing or additional information before being approved. Borrowers tend to become anxious while waiting for an approval but don't read too much into delays and requests for more information, it is a natural part of the approval process. However, the adage *the squeaky wheel gets the grease* applies here. Maintaining regular communication with your loan officer will help insure your application is attended to as promptly as possible.

The underwriting department will order an appraisal of the property you want to purchase unless a recent one is already available. The lender will also require a title report, which your attorney will usually order so that title insurance may be obtained. Title insurance protects you and the lender as it insures the property you are buying is free from defects or liens unless listed as allowable exceptions in the title report.

Loan officers and underwriters have supervisors. Of course, loan officers will not be happy if you take an end run around them but in rare circumstances it may be necessary to speak with someone else at your bank. If you are facing challenges in dealing with your loan officer or experiencing unreasonable delays in getting approval, ask for a supervisor. Don't be afraid to speak up if you feel something has gone awry, sometimes being proactive can move things along. I have done this when agreed upon deadlines for approvals were missed. If you have a relationship with the branch manager, even though they do not deal with the loan process, they may be able to make a call on your behalf to expedite the process if you run into any roadblocks. Knowing this allows you to work up the chain of authorization if you need to.

Honesty counts. Banks will accept but verify what you tell them. They will also ask for documentation to support your income such as tax returns, bank statements, w2's from your employer and lots more if you are self-employed. Honesty is the best policy, don't try to fudge the numbers. A lie on an application is not only illegal, but if discovered it will surely leave you without an approval.

HOW LONG DOES APPROVAL TAKE?

The process of loan approval varies from lender to lender but thirty to sixty days under normal circumstances is reasonable. Getting pre-qualified reduces the chances of major surprises while waiting for a credit decision. The process will certainly take longer if you are slow in providing the lender with information they have requested. For this reason, plus the fact your attorney needs time to gather title searches and other documents, you should allow enough time in your purchase contract to get all these things done without applying pressure to your moving plans.

MORTGAGE POSITIONS

A property can have more than one loan placed upon it. The order in which each loan would be paid in a legal proceeding such as a default or bankruptcy would be based upon the loan's *position*. If a legal battle should arise, the *noteholders* or lenders would have different rights based on their position. The first loan *recorded* with the County Clerk's office would be in the first position. The first position is also more commonly referred to as a *first mortgage*. Recording a loan makes it part of the public record and puts other potential lenders on notice that the property is already *encumbered* or has a debt associated with it.

Additional loans would fall in line with a *second mortgage* being *subordinate* to the first and so forth down the list. This legal distinction is different from and outweighs the order in which you might borrow or repay money under normal circumstances. In rare instances, a noteholder's position may improve or deteriorate, meaning be moved up or down in pecking order of position if the parties agree to do so. More commonly a noteholder's position will change or move up if a loan ahead of it is paid off.

Banks and most other lenders like to lend in the first position and sometimes insist upon it. The first position provides a much higher degree of likelihood that some portion of the outstanding loan, or the entire loan balance, will be paid off in the event of a default, even if there are not enough funds to pay all the outstanding debts.

THE BIG SWITCH

You should know that as part of the process of underwriting your loan and after you have received a loan, the bank may sell that loan to another bank or financial institution at any time. While all the terms within your loan will remain the same, you may be asked to send your payment somewhere else. Banks make loans to make profits, but they also sell loans to raise cash, so they can write more loans. The truth is banks can make more on upfront fees than they can by servicing or collecting your loan payments over many years. So, don't be surprised if your local lender sells your loan to someone else.

FINAL NOTE ABOUT BANKS

To eliminate surprises and understand what you are signing up for when borrowing money, always ask questions. But ask open ended questions, such as "Are there any other fees?" Also restate the question in a different form such as "Are there any other expenses I need to prepare for?" "What other costs might be associated with this loan?"

When you get an answer to your question, never assume you have received a complete answer and follow up with "Anything else?" "Are you sure?" Often you will jog a person's memory or give them a chance to add something they have omitted. Often the answer is something to the effect of "Well, you will have your normal *closing costs*."

Obviously if this is your first home, you probably don't know what normal closing costs are, but the banker who does this everyday assumes you do and that can become a hidden expense for you when the time comes to finalize a loan.

My Mom taught me to constantly try to find out what you don't know, that's how you avoid misunderstandings and surprises. Don't be afraid to ask, you are making a very long-term commitment when you take out a mortgage on a home.

CHAPTER 13
CALCULATING LOAN COSTS

SHOPPING FOR A MORTGAGE

When shopping for a mortgage, an often-overlooked factor to consider, aside from the interest rate which most people focus on, is the *term*, or length of the loan. Many home buyers are led to believe the thirty-year or even forty-year loans are the best way to go because they have the lowest monthly payments.

Long term loans also increase the amount you can borrow because you are committing to a longer repayment period with similar monthly payments. However, market interest rates are also higher on longer term loans to factor in additional risks such as a longer period for potential non-payment and changing interest rates. The pitfall not discussed, is that you have very little equity buildup for quite a while in longer term loans than shorter term loans.

Use Google or another search engine to find a *mortgage calculator*. You will be able to input the amount of a loan, the interest rate and term to see what your payments will be. By changing the information entered, you will be able to compare the results of different terms and interest rates. Being able to change the amount borrowed or down payment will also let you tinker with what happens when you change the amount of capital you are investing. I have included examples of mortgage calculations below that demonstrate significant variations in cost between 15-year and 30-year loans.

As a percentage of your total monthly payment, interest is only a portion of what you are paying. As noted earlier, almost all mortgages made through banks have payments that include four components Principal, Interest, Taxes, and Insurance (*PITI*). *Principal* is the amount of money that reduces your balance and becomes your equity in the property while *Interest* is the banks income, *Taxes* are our governments cut and the *Insurance* protects your investment as well as the banks collateral.

Consider this example:

Value of House: $100,000
Mortgage: $75,000
Interest Rate: 5%
Term: 30 years
Taxes: $5,000 per year
Insurance: $1,200 per year

The monthly loan payment would look like this:

$90.00	Principal Payment
$313.00	Interest Payment
$416.67	Taxes ($5,000 / 12)
$100.00	Insurance ($1,200 / 12)
$919.67	**TOTAL MONTHLY PAYMENT**

In this example, as with most fixed rate loans, the monthly payment of principal and interest you send to the bank stays the same throughout the term of the loan, but the amount of principal paid off increases and the interest on the lower remaining balance is reduced with each payment. For the first payment, the interest paid represents 34% of the total payment (Interest of $313.00 divided by $919.67 Total Payment).

The next table shows payment without taxes and insurance because these monies go into an escrow account, to be paid on your behalf. The bank only uses $403 noted in the column marked "payment" to pay the loan off, even though you send the much larger monthly payment of $919.67 in this example.

360 Payments	Pymt.	Principal	Int.	Balance
1 (1 Month)	$403	$90	$313	$74,910
12 (1 Year)	$403	$94	$308	$73,893
24 (2 Years)	$403	$99	$303	$72,730
36 (3 Years)	$403	$104	$298	$71,508
48 (4 Years)	$403	$110	$293	$70,222
60 (5 Years)	$403	$115	$287	$68,871
72 (6 Years)	$403	$121	$282	$67,451
84 (7 Years)	$403	$127	$275	$65,958
96 (8 Years)	$403	$134	$269	$64,389
108 (9 Years)	$403	$141	$262	$62,740
120 (10 Years)	$403	$148	$255	$61,006
180 (15 Years)	$403	$190	$213	$50,912
240 (20 Years)	$403	$243	$159	$37,958
300 (25 Years)	$403	$312	$90	$21,333
360 (30 Years)	$403	$398	$2	$0

15 YEAR TERM

In the same example used above, if we cut the term from 30 years to 15 years here is what happens to the monthly payments:

Value of House: $100,000
Mortgage: $75,000
Interest Rate: 5%
Term: 15 years
Taxes: $5,000 per year
Insurance: $1,200 per year

The monthly loan payment would look like this:

$281.00	Principal Payment
$313.00	Interest Payment
$416.67	Taxes ($5,000 / 12)
$100.00	Insurance ($1,200 / 12)
$1,110.67	**TOTAL MONTHLY PAYMENT**

For the first payment, the interest paid represents 28.2% of the total payment (Interest of $313.00 divided by $1,110.67 Total Payment).

180 Payments		Pymt	Principal	Int.	Balance
1	(1 Month)	$593	$281	$313	$74,719
12	(1 Year)	$593	$294	$299	$71,555
24	(2 Years)	$593	$309	$284	$67,933
36	(3 Years)	$593	$325	$269	$64,126
48	(4 Years)	$593	$341	$252	$60,124
60	(5 Years)	$593	$359	$234	$55,918
72	(6 Years)	$593	$377	$216	$51,496
84	(7 Years)	$593	$396	$197	$46,848
96	(8 Years)	$593	$417	$177	$41,963
108	(9 Years)	$593	$438	$155	$36,827
120	(10 Years)	$593	$460	$133	$31,429
150	(12.5Years)	$593	$521	$72	$16,693
180	(15 Years)	$593	$591	$2	$0

In this example notice how quickly the principal diminishes in the last five years, it drops from $31,429 to $0 in five years, so I inserted a 12.5-year row to highlight how fast the remaining principal is paid off in the end. Also, notice your change in equity build up. For a 30-year loan, at the 60th payment (fifth year), the balance due is $68,871 compared to $55,918 for the 60th payment (fifth year) on a 15-year loan. At the 120th payment (tenth year), the 30-year loan balance is $61,006 compared to $31,429 on a 15-year loan.

EQUITY BUILD UP

This means if you decided to get out of your investment after 5 years, you would have accumulated $12,953 more in equity on a 15-year loan than a 30-year loan (Remaining balance of $68,871 minus $55,918). If you decided to get out of your investment after 10 years, you would have accumulated $29,577 more equity on a 15-year loan than on a 30-year loan (Remaining balance $61,006 minus $31,429). I know reading the numbers might be confusing so here they are in another format:

BALANCE DUE AFTER 5 YEARS	
30 Year Loan	15 Year Loan
at 60th Payment	at 60th Payment
Principal Paid $6,129	Principal Paid $19,082
Balance Due $68,871	Balance Due $55,918
Difference in Equity $68,871 minus $55,918 = **$12,953**	

After five years, you will have an equity buildup of **$12,953** which by itself is a 51.8% return on your original $25,000 down payment.

BALANCE DUE AFTER 10 YEARS	
30 Year Loan	15 Year Loan
at 120th Payment	at 120th Payment
Principal Paid $13,994	Principal Paid $43,571
Balance Due $61,006	Balance Due $31,429
Difference in Equity $61,006 minus $31,429 = **$29,577**	

After ten years, you will have an equity buildup of **$29,577** which by itself is a 118.3% return on your original $25,000 down payment.

Time flies and before you know it the years have passed. If you can purchase a home now with a fifteen-year mortgage, it will be free and clear when you make that 180th payment. All yours, debt free, but more importantly, the money that was being used to pay off your loan will become free to use for anything you desire.

The important point is that with a 15-year loan you have a lot more to show for your effort in a shorter amount of time without accounting for the benefits of appreciation you may have accrued. If you cannot afford the payments for a 15-year loan, do the math on a 20-year loan or a 25-year loan instead of taking a traditional 30-year loan. This way you will still be able to derive substantial savings.

As previously noted, rates are lower for short term loans, so for a better comparison of savings compared to a 30-year loan, it would be fair to use a 4.5% interest rate with a 15-year term, which would look like this:

> Value of House: $100,000
> Mortgage: $75,000
> Interest Rate: 4.5%
> Term: 15 years
> Taxes: $5,000 per year
> Insurance: $1,200 per year

The monthly loan payment would look like this:

$292.00	Principal Payment
$281.00	Interest Payment
$416.67	Taxes ($5,000 / 12)
$100.00	Insurance ($1,200 / 12)
$1,089.67	TOTAL MONTHLY PAYMENT

For the first payment, the interest paid represents 25.8% of the total payment (Interest of $281.00 divided by $1,089.67 Total Payment). Here are the payments side by side:

30 YEAR TERM **$75,000 @ 5%**	15 YEAR TERM **$75,000 @ 4.5%**
$90.00 Principal payment	$292.00 Principal payment
$313.00 Interest Payment	$281.00 Interest Payment
$416.67 Taxes ($5,000 / 12)	$416.67 Taxes ($5,000 / 12)
$100.00 Insurance ($1,200 / 12)	$100.00 Insurance ($1,200 / 12)
$919.67 **TOTAL PAYMENT**	**$1,089.67** **TOTAL PAYMENT**
$69,941.84 TOTAL INTEREST PAID	$28,274.09 TOTAL INTEREST PAID
$144,941.84 PYMTS W/ PRINCIPAL	$103,274.09 PYMTS W/ PRINCIPAL

In these examples, there is a $170 per month payment difference to pay off the property in 15 years instead of 30 years. Also, note the huge difference in total interest paid and total payments made including principal.

INTEREST ADDS UP

For longer term loans the total amount of interest you pay increases exponentially. Here are some examples of the interest to be paid on a $100,000 loan for the number of years shown without principal repayments.

INTEREST ONLY:

YEARS	5%	6%	7%
10 years	$27,278.62	$33,224.60	$39,330.18
15 years	$42,342.85	$51,894.23	$61,789.09
20 years	$58,389.38	$71,943.45	$86,071.74
25 years	$75,377.01	$93,290.42	$112,033.76
30 years	$93,255.78	$115,838.19	$139,508.90
40 years	$131,454.37	$164,102.55	$198,287.01

MORTGAGE ESCROW ACCOUNT

When a bank is going to be paying bills such as real estate taxes or insurance on your behalf, it will set up an escrow account. Each month the bank will deposit a portion of your monthly payment earmarked for escrow payments into this account and pay the bills from these funds when they become due.

Because the amount of the bills paid from an escrow account can change over time, adjustments are made, usually annually. This ensures the bank will always have the funds anticipated to be paid for your bills on hand in advance. These escrow payments will become a part of your mortgage payment. Lenders also like to escrow for the taxes, so they know they are paid promptly to prevent a lien being placed on the property for unpaid taxes. If the bank is not paying these expenses, be sure that you are.

Some mortgage calculators allow you to input taxes and insurance as well. Sometimes you can even add a starting payment date and other information for a more personalized result. Today this is easy to do. In the old days, I used a little book with tables of rates and terms that I needed to reference, then calculate the insurance and taxes manually and add it all up to calculate the mortgage payment.

BI-WEEKLY PAYMENT OPTION

In addition to ALWAYS borrowing using shorter term loans, there are two other great ways to pay down your mortgage more quickly and save interest expense. One way is to accelerate your payments using a bi-weekly payment instead of a monthly payment. If you make payments every two weeks, you will be making twenty-six payments a year (52 weeks divided by 2 = 26 payments). Your biweekly payments of principal and interest will be about half of a monthly mortgage payment, but you will make more of them and reduce the principal faster. This reduces your overall interest as well.

Consider this example:
Value of House: $100,000
Mortgage: $75,000
Interest Rate: 5%
Term: 30 years (BI-WEEKLY=26 PAYMENTS)
Taxes: $5,000 per year
Insurance: $1,200 per year

A comparison of the bi-weekly and monthly loan payments would look like this:

BI-WEEKLY (26 Payments)		MONTHLY (12 Payments)
$201.31 Principal & Interest		$403.00 Principal & Interest
$192.31 Taxes ($5,000 / 26)		$416.67 Taxes ($5,000 / 12)
$ 46.15 Insurance ($1,200 / 26)		$100.00 Insurance ($1,200 / 12)
$439.77 TOTAL PAYMENT		**$919.67 TOTAL PAYMENT**
$72.40 Average Interest Per Payment		$194.28 Average Interest Per Payment
Bi-Weekly = $11,434.02 Annual Payments ($439.77 x 26)		
Monthly = $11,036.04 Annual Payments ($919.67 x 12)		
Total Interest Paid:		
Bi-Weekly = $56,616.64		
Monthly = $69,941.84		

You would pay off the loan in about 25 years instead of 30 years with a bi-weekly payment plan vs a traditional 30-year loan, saving you 5 years of payments and interest expense totaling $13,325.20. ($69,941.84 - $56,616.64 = $13,325.20)

THIRTEEN IS A LUCKY NUMBER

Well, it may not always be lucky for everyone, but in some cultures, it is. One thing is for sure, if you make thirteen mortgage payments a year on a loan instead of twelve, this is another method you can use to save thousands of dollars in interest over the life of a loan.

Conceptually, making thirteen annual payments is very much like the bi-weekly plan outlined above, but because the payments are made more often in the bi-weekly plan, the compounding effect of the interest rate on the loan is greater when compared to making thirteen payments. The thirteenth payment is an excellent option for anyone who gets an annual bonus. When you have the extra cash in hand, use some of it to make an extra principal payment each year and you will see similar results in acceleration of your pay-off date and reductions in the amount of interest you pay.

CHAPTER 14
OPM

If you are not going to be using your own money, then you will be using *OPM* or *Other People's Money*, which is simply any money you can raise that is not yours. This includes borrowing from family, friends, sellers, banks, credit unions and any other type of lending institution or source you can think of.

Unless you have lots of cash, using other people's money is the best way to acquire your first home.

LEVERAGE THROUGH BORROWING
Here are some examples of the differences between using all your money, rather than some of your money, and finally, little to none of your money when purchasing a property.

Example 1A:
In an all cash deal of $100,000 where you put up 100% of the money and the property you bought appreciated 10% in a year, you would have a profit or a capital gain of $10,000, with an ROI of 10%.

Example 2A:
If you put 25% or $25,000 down and borrowed the balance of the money at 5% from a bank, then the same profit of $10,000 in example 1A would be

reduced by the interest expense on the $75,000 you borrowed. The 5% interest would cost you $3,750 in the first year, so your appreciation or profit would now be $6,250. Even though the $6,250 is fewer total dollars than netted in example 1A, remember your investment in this example is only $25,000. Therefore, $6,250 is a 25% ROI calculated as ($6,250 divided by $25,000 down payment).

Example 3A:

If you put 10% or $10,000 down and borrowed the balance of the money at 5% from a bank, then the same appreciation or profit of $10,000 would be reduced by the interest expense on $90,000. The 5% interest would cost you $4,500 in the first year, so your profit would be $5,500. Your investment is now only $10,000, so $5,500 equals a 55% return on your investment ($5,550 divided by $10,000 down payment).

Example 4A:

If you put no money down on a $100,000 home and borrowed the $100,000 at 5% from a bank, then the same appreciation or profit of $10,000 would be reduced by the interest expense on $100,000. The 5% interest would cost you $5,000 in the first year, so your profit would be $5,000. Your investment was zero so $5,000 is your gain without risking any capital.

This is the super power of leverage related to borrowing money! This exponential growth of your return as a percentage of your down payment is one of the primary reasons real estate is such an attractive wealth building vehicle. As you earn more money in relationship to your total investment, the higher your *Return on Investment* (*ROI*) will be.

By using other people's money, you increase the leverage on your money and therefore increase your potential ROI. Do not let the numbers fool you, the difference between a ten percent return and a twenty percent return is not ten percent, it is a one hundred percent increase or a doubling of your 10% return to 20%. Greater appreciation combined with leverage from borrowing can create even larger gains.

Here is how a greater rise in real estate values would affect your equity using the same example of a $100,000 purchase price which has appreciated 20%. The value of the home would now be $120,000.

Example 1B:
In an all cash deal of $100,000 where you put up 100% of the money and the property you bought appreciated 20% in a year, you would have a profit or a capital gain of $20,000 or an ROI of 20% ($20,000 divided by $100,000).

Example 2B:
If you put 25% or $25,000 down and borrowed the balance of the money at 5% from a bank, then the same gain of $20,000 on a $100,000 house would be reduced by the interest expense on the $75,000 you borrowed. The 5% interest would cost you $3,750 in the first year, so your net gain would now be $16,250. Even though the $16,250 is less dollars than the $20,000 netted in example 1B, remember your investment in this example is only $25,000, so $16,250 now equals a **65% return on your investment** ($16,250 divided by $25,000 down payment).

Example 3B:
If you put 10% or $10,000 down and borrowed the balance of the money at 5% from a bank, then the same appreciation of $20,000 would be reduced by the interest expense on $90,000. The 5% interest would cost you $4,500 in the first year, so your profit would be $15,500. Your investment is now only $10,000, so $15,500 equals a **155% return on your investment** ($15,500 divided by $25,000 down payment).

Example 4B:
If you put no money down on a $100,000 home and borrowed the $100,000 at 5% from a bank, then the same appreciation of $20,000 would be reduced by the interest expense on $100,000. The 5% interest would cost you $5,000 in the first year,

so your profit would be $15,000. Your investment was zero so $15,000 is your gain without risking any capital.

BE PRUDENT

A word of caution; you can over leverage yourself if you borrow more than you can afford to repay or lose your source of income, even if it is a somewhat temporary setback. Markets change and will provide different rates of appreciation or depreciation over time. Therefore, understanding your market before you buy is a critical component of planning.

If you cannot meet your monthly debt payments, you could incur large expenses or even lose your property in a legal action, bankruptcy or foreclosure proceeding. **Prudent borrowing is of paramount importance.** If you default on your debt and agreements, you can also lose the ability to borrow in the future.

Please note, these examples do not include the costs of *closing* a loan which could include fees and other upfront charges because these costs can range from zero on a personal loan to whatever terms you negotiate with a lender. However, you may derive tax benefits from many of these additional costs. Some of your closing costs may be written off in the current year, while others will be *amortized* or spread out over the life of the loan, or *useful life* of the property, as defined by the IRS for accounting purposes.

INFLATION

Inflation and appreciation cause the prices of properties to increase over time. By owning a home that appreciates, you leverage inflation or hedge against it, to create greater wealth for yourself. While you are building equity, anyone who is not invested in assets such as real estate that appreciates is losing buying power on their dollars along the way.

As a tenant, one of the biggest arguments against renting, aside from the tax deductions on interest expense and pride of ownership, is the appreciation that is a lost opportunity in the rental market.

Rents are a transfer of money that erode personal wealth for tenants while increasing personal wealth for landlords.

INTEREST

In these examples, for simplicity, only the first year of interest is used to demonstrate the effect of leverage. In each of the following years as your loan is paid down, the declining interest expense will leave you with increasingly more profits as you get closer to the day your loan is paid off.

While borrowing gives you leverage, and interest is deductible, keeping the cost of interest down is still important because it is potential profit dollars being expensed. There is a positive aspect to be found in paying interest charges; the government will share in the cost of your interest expense because you can claim it as a tax deduction against your other income. Your net ROI will be higher if you factor in this tax deduction, which can reduce your taxable income based on your income tax bracket.

As noted in chapter thirteen, using shorter term loans such as fifteen years instead of thirty years or making payments every four weeks instead of monthly are ways to mitigate the overall interest you will pay while balancing the maximum potential of leverage and the costs of interest.

SELLER'S MONEY

Sometimes sellers are willing to hold a mortgage or *note*, and this can be the easiest way to obtain financing. You may also be able to negotiate a better interest rate than banks are offering if you are dealing directly with the seller. When shopping, be sure to inquire if any properties are on the market with *seller financing* as an option. Seller financing should also reduce your closing costs because several of the bank's fees are eliminated.

Seller financing is less personal than going to family and friends and may be much cheaper than using a bank. You are probably going to be approved if you can come up with an agreed upon down payment.

Not every seller needs the cash from a sale. Dealing directly with sellers is also the easiest way to buy a home without your own money, if you are fortunate enough to find a seller offering a *"no money down"* deal with seller financing.

ASSUMABLE LOANS

An *assumable loan* is an existing debt on a property that you can take over or continue to make the payments for until the loan is paid in full. Assuming an existing loan also allows you to bypass the costs associated with getting your own loan. Assumption is usually a simple task and bears minimal cost. Some assumable loans require the lender's approval while others do not. If the terms are favorable, this is a great way to acquire some debt. Most banks do not offer assumable loans, but private sellers are more likely to and some FHA and VA loans are assumable. A seller should know if the loan they have on their home is assumable, therefore it never hurts to ask!

Depending on the remaining balance of an assumable loan, you might be able to put down the remainder of the purchase price for the property or you could supplement your deposit with some additional financing from another source to make the deal. The original *note holder* or lender may even be willing to increase the amount of the loan if they find the deal to be worthwhile. Again, it never hurts to ask!

FAMILY AND FRIENDS
When you borrow from family and friends, should you pay interest? Yes, you should pay a fair rate, which I often find falls between the rate being earned in a savings account or other investment and what you would have to pay a bank.

For example, right now savings rates are around 1% and investment grade bonds are about 3%, while banks' lending rates are about 4 to 5%. In this scenario, I think paying 3% to 5% is a fair rate. At 4% this is a win-win, you will also save the closing costs, time and hassle associated with applying for loans. The lender makes some extra money and you save some.

When you seek long terms loans, it is harder for a lender to know what a fair rate will be. If you find someone is willing to make a long-term loan at a low interest rate, it can make your home purchase an even sweeter home sweet home.

Family and friends are also good sources for short term money. If your parents can help you out, they may be willing to make the long-term investment with you, probably without a loan application. Since most of us are not in the business of lending like banks, the concept of lending money for a short period of time will often be more palatable than a longer-term commitment. This path may allow you to close on a purchase quickly with reduced costs. You could then place more traditional longer-term financing on a property from a bank or other source after you are settled in.

CO-SIGNERS

Using a co-signer to obtain a loan from a bank or other party is not the same as borrowing their money, but it could morph into that. A co-signer *pledges* to pay your loan if you fail to do so. Therefore, asking someone to co-sign a loan for you is tantamount to asking them for a loan in terms of risk to the co-signer.

So why would someone take on this risk for you? Because they know you better than the bank or lender and know you are "good for the money". They believe you would never allow them to become responsible for your debt and so they are willing to stand up for you and offer additional assurance to a lender that you ARE good for the money. Here again, parents are often most willing to do this to help their children achieve their dreams of home ownership, but there may be others in the wings that you might approach to lend credibility to your loan application as a co-signer.

You also may have other collateral or assets such as a vehicle, a retirement fund, insurance policy or something which you could pledge to a co-signer that a lender would not or could not accept while considering the approval of your application.

PRIVATE MONEY

Most of us think of a mortgage as a loan from a bank because it commonly is. Yet thousands and thousands of real estate transactions occur daily, many of which use *Private Mortgage Money*. The difference between private mortgage money and a personal loan is that the mortgage is recorded to protect the lender. Private money or personal loans can be evidenced by a *promissory note*, which even though it is not recorded, is still a legal document.

The company you work for might even be an unlikely source for a loan. Large companies sometimes have programs to finance homes for employees relocating.

RENTAL INCOME

Buying a *Mother/Daughter* style home with an *accessory apartment* or a multi-family home could allow you to create an income opportunity. Purchasing an income producing property may allow you to afford home ownership that might not otherwise be possible, or you may just want the extra income. If you are going to venture into being a landlord/home owner, be sure to check that it is legal to rent the property you are considering with the local authorities before committing to buy. In many towns there are restrictions and/or rental permit requirements which may prevent you from renting some or all your property.

NO MONEY DOWN

"No-money down" financing means transferring title or ownership without cash, although some form of *good and valuable consideration* must change hands to create a contract of sale. You may, however, still have other out of pocket expenses such as closing costs, back taxes that need to be paid, or rehabilitation costs that you will incur. Therefore, a "no money down" transaction is generally a misnomer in the sense that it does not mean you will not need any money at all.

It is true that many properties do change hands with "no-money down", and I have even bought a home myself without making a cash down payment, by offering other *valuable consideration.* However, the concept of purchasing property with no money is not as easy as some people would have you believe.

"No-money down" deals are typically financed by a seller who will hold a mortgage for the full amount of the sale. There are also a few government programs that are discussed in the chapter titled *Types of Loans* that will finance from 96.5% to 100% of a home's price if you qualify.

Having said this, you should understand that in every market there may be distressed properties which are difficult to sell, and that some owners might consider "no money down" offers. In some fully developed markets, there may also be too many homes available for sale and some sellers would rather take a "no money down" deal instead of reducing their asking price drastically or having to remain in the market for an extended period, potentially resulting in years of trying to sell.

As time passes, some sellers wear down, they get tired of showing their home repeatedly or arguably worse, not at all. Some sellers become so pressured financially to get out of a property that a "no money down" deal which preserves some of their equity or gets them out from under their debt is enough motivation for them to sell. In this scenario, it would be better to collect some return of money over time than losing everything by continuing to hold a property that one cannot afford to cover the carrying costs on.

If a seller is offering financing, you might convince them to accept a "no money down" offer. Typically, you will not be able to negotiate the best pricing under these circumstances. Having said this, you should still attempt to negotiate the best price you can. You also need to negotiate a reasonable interest rate to be sure a deal makes economic sense.

No-money down transactions often occur in three common formats:

- Owner Holds a *Note* or a Mortgage.

- Owner Holds a *Second Mortgage.*
  (See Chapter 14)

- Owner Accepts Something Other Than
  Money as Payment.

Item three is essentially a *barter transaction,* where you give something other than money for a down payment. In another one of my books titled **Barter Your Way to Greater Wealth,** I describe in detail how I purchased a house without cash by bartering for it. I found a bank that accepted what I bartered in lieu of a cash down payment and gave me a mortgage for the balance owed. I then renovated much of the house and property by bartering for the things I needed.

If you have something of value that a seller would accept instead of cash, you could create your own barter transaction. You are only going to be limited by your imagination when it comes to striking a barter deal.

Some of the common reasons a seller would sell without a down payment:

- The seller is in imminent risk of foreclosure and would rather convert their equity into a mortgage, than lose all of it in a foreclosure proceeding.

- The seller owes back taxes which they cannot pay, and the taxes are accruing everyday they own the property. This is a way out from under their debt. In some instances, the buyer may agree to pay the back taxes as part of or as the entire sales price. In these cases, it could mean no money to the seller, but the buyer would still have to outlay some cash to satisfy the back taxes. If the back taxes were already converted to a lien on the property, then the deed could not be transferred until the taxes were paid by either party, so this could become a *condition of sale.*

- If a seller is experiencing very high carrying costs that they cannot cover, and the negative cash flow will cause substantial financial losses, then selling with no-money down can be a viable option.

- Sellers can ask higher listing prices. Many potential buyers with credit issues that prevent them from getting a traditional loan with a bank are willing to pay more in price, if the seller will give them the loan.

- Most sellers need or want the money from the sale of their real estate, but not all. Some sellers may not want the income at the current time but want to sell the property. An *installment sale*, or payout over time by the seller holding a mortgage can help the seller to defer tax liability.

- Distressed properties that have problems or have been on the market for a long time are candidates for sellers to unload by offering attractive owner financing.

CHAPTER 15

USING YOUR MONEY

Most first-time home buyers try to put down somewhere between twenty and thirty percent. If you put less than 20% down on a home, you may incur another expense because your lender may require *private mortgage insurance (PMI)* to protect their investment. This is why most banks ask for and borrowers put down 20% or more. If you have the resources, you may be tempted to pay all cash but wait! Have you done the return on your investment calculation to determine if that is the best use for your cash.

On my first home I took the traditional route with a moderate down payment and a conventional loan. When I started investing in real estate I used as little of my own money as possible but now I buy for all cash. Depending on your circumstances either strategy or something in the middle can work for you. Buying all cash provides some peace of mind knowing you will not have to worry about making mortgage payments. Foreclosure in tough times is also never a consideration if there is no loan attached to a property. Having 100% equity also will allow you to either take out a home equity line of credit whenever you may need to. You could also apply for a mortgage in the future if you wanted to finance the property.

If retirement is within reach, moving into a new home without having to make monthly payments can make life simpler.

CASH

In the current economic climate, interest rates are relatively low. When I started buying real estate, interest rates were in the double digits. I knew people who had mortgage rates of 16% and in 1981 some mortgage rates were over 18%. If you are fortunate enough to have cash to purchase a home, then you need to weigh the benefits of using your own money against borrowing from others.

Cash is a *liquid asset* and the ease in which you can convert other assets to cash speaks to their level of *liquidity* or its opposite, *illiquidity*. Money locked up in a CD to obtain a higher savings rate than a money market account is liquid because you can close the CD very easily and remove the cash. This is also true of stocks and bonds that can be sold or liquidated with a phone call to your broker or a few taps on a keyboard if you manage your own brokerage account. You may incur some cost to achieve liquidity, but this will be insignificant compared to the time and costs required to convert illiquid assets such as real estate into cash.

Real estate is not considered a liquid investment because it fails the litmus test of being able to liquidate quickly at the market value. It can take months or years to sell a property if you are trying to achieve a sale at market prices, depending on many external factors you cannot control. If you needed cash in ten days, it is highly unlikely you would be able to offer a property for sale, find a buyer and receive the proceeds. After having an accepted offer, the time it will take till you have the cash in hand can easily be more than sixty days. Even with an all cash offer, it usually takes attorneys a few weeks to obtain the information they need to prepare for a closing and schedule an agreeable date with all the parties involved.

If you have your own cash available, you can save quite a bit of money by eliminating closing costs such as the mortgage tax, the banks attorney fees, points and or origination fees and the other fees banks build into closing costs. You will also enjoy significant savings from not having to pay interest. Combined, these factors should give you better returns than you are getting in other investments.

As an example, when I bought my most recent home, mortgage interest rates were under 3% for a mortgage and the liquid investments I had were earning over 5%. The spread was large enough for me not to liquidate these holdings and incur capital gains taxes. By borrowing, I would also get to write off the 3% interest so my effective spread in the rates is greater from a tax perspective. I have also freed up my working funds for the long term, which I expect to do significantly better with in terms of income from my future cash investments.

Therefore, lower taxes, interest rates, achievable rates of return and liquidity are the driving forces which determine if you should use your own money. Each case is unique, and your decision should be made based on your financial condition.

Another important factor to monitor is the direction in which interest rates are heading. Since they bottomed out after the last financial market meltdown, interest rates have really had no place to go but up. While it is true that many people expected rates to rise much more quickly than they did, the government has artificially maintained low rates to help shore up the economy. Eventually, the market will adjust as changes in financial policy occur.

If you have cash and use it to leverage a lower price, which often can save you a significant amount of money, you might want to take advantage of the opportunity. I purchased a house with an asking price of $129,000 for $100,000 cash because the sellers previous two contracts, which were much closer to the asking price, both fell through because the buyers couldn't obtain the financing. After many months of delays the seller had enough and decided to accept my offer rather than holding out for a better offer. The seller got an iron clad deal for all cash from me rather than a clause of "subject to buyer obtaining financing" or "subject to buyer selling their home". After completing the purchase, I could then place financing on the home if I wanted too.

Another advantage of an all cash purchase is the sale can *close* faster because you are not waiting on a bank's approval and having to meet all their requirements. This may make you the best option for a seller. Bidding wars are often avoided because the competition must raise the amount they borrow to make a higher offer. You can usually close or transfer the deed to your name as soon as your attorney receives a *clean title report*. A clean or clear title means there are no liens or encumbrances on the property. Therefore, you can buy a home cheaper, when sellers need to get out fast.

Homeowner's insurance is required by lenders to repair or replace your home if an insured loss occurs, which protects you and the lenders investment. Therefore, this type of insurance is not required if you do not have a loan secured by your home. It would however be risky not to insure a home without a mortgage because that would mean all your capital would be at risk. Being self-insured is rarely a good idea unless you have significant resources to absorb a loss and even then, it is generally considered a bad bet to go uninsured.

An appraisal and a home inspection are also not required when buying a home for all cash. If you have done enough research and compared asking prices and selling prices of comparable properties, the appraisal cost might be an expense you can forgo. If you are familiar with home construction and are comfortable doing your own inspection you could save some money here too. If not, it would be wise to get an independent appraisal and inspection.

CASH PURCHASE TAX DEDUCTIONS

People often ask if they get a tax deduction or write off when buying a house all cash. The answer is no. The cost of a home, including any improvements, is not tax deductible, only the interest, real estate taxes, and some expenses are. Deductible rules are subject to changes in the tax law, as we have seen recently with the capping of real estate taxes at $10,000 for Federal income tax deduction purposes on your personal residence or residences. Properties held for business purposes are not subjected to this limitation.

As noted a few chapters earlier, when you sell your primary residence, you will be entitled to an exemption from taxes on the first $250,000 in profit you have made or $500,000 if you are married filing a joint tax return. You must have lived in the house for two of the previous five years from the selling date to qualify for this exemption.

**You are entitled to take this deduction
once every two years
for as many times as you like.**

If you own more than one home, your primary residence or legal residence for tax purposes is the house you live in most of the year. In the simplest sense your profit is calculated as the *base price* of the house which is what you paid for it plus some of your closing costs, plus certain types of improvements you have made to the property over the years.

HOME EQUITY LOAN
The more money you put down on your home the greater your equity in the property will be. If you are concerned about tying up too much of your extra cash and only putting the minimum down, then you may want to consider the option of making a larger down payment and applying for a home equity line of credit. This is a great way to enjoy the savings of lower interest payments, which will allow you to build even greater equity in your home, while still being able to borrow against the home if you really need the money back for another purpose.

The primary difference between taking a larger mortgage versus a credit line is you only use the credit line when you need it, so if you never use it interest doesn't accrue, and you have no costs. The process to apply for an equity line is also much easier and far less expensive than applying for a mortgage.

A home equity credit line also provides a sense of security giving you time to rebuild your cash reserves if you have no unexpected expenses and allow the home equity line to remain dormant. The great thing about this type of loan is you are pre-approved and often have a revolving credit line valid for up to twenty years. You can also increase the amount of your credit line as the value of your home appreciates or you pay more of the principal off over time. This is a great solution to reducing potential illiquidity from putting extra cash into a home.

CHAPTER 16
CALCULATING CLOSING COSTS

ONLY YOU CAN CALCULATE HOW MUCH YOU CAN AFFORD TO SPEND WHEN PURCHASING A HOME

SO, WHAT CAN YOU AFFORD?

You need to make an honest and realistic assessment of how much you can afford to spend for or invest in your dream home. To make a decision that is right for you, you must understand your finances, your tolerance for risk and allow something for unexpected expenses in your budget. Do you have enough personal income or liquid assists to carry your purchase if necessary? This means have you allowed enough reserves in your calculations to carry you through tough times if you lost your job or became ill for a short period of time.

I have always made important financial investment decisions by considering the *worst-case scenario* from a financial perspective. I ask myself, how will I manage to pay for this if everything goes wrong in a perfect storm of setbacks? Many first-time home buyers are blinded by their emotions, causing them to overlook or minimize potential risks. This can prevent you from considering the worst-case scenario as a possibility. You need to ground yourself emotionally to prevent yourself from rushing into what could turn into a bad deal. If your worst-case scenario is palatable, then go for it!

THIS IS A BIG DEAL

Buying your dream home is a big deal. It requires lots of due diligence to determine if a home is right for you. You will need to ask a lot of questions. Who should you listen to; your broker, the seller, your lawyer, banker, or accountant? The answer is all of them can provide you with advice, but only you can determine if a home is right for you.

All the professionals around you can educate you, allowing you to expand your knowledge base, because each has different life experience and professional expertise. What they cannot provide you with is the guts, gumption, or chutzpah to take the plunge and sign on the dotted line, because when the dust settles, after you have closed the deal, the work and risk falls to you alone.

Russell Simmons is credited with saying **"Surround yourself with people who are smarter than you"**. By this he didn't necessarily mean more intelligent, but he did mean more experienced or able to do a better job than you in a specific area of expertise to achieve a more successful outcome.

You should also always remain acutely aware of the fact that even though professionals may have your best interests at heart, not all professionals are equally trained or experienced and even the best can have a bad day. Lawyers and accountants may specialize in areas outside of the world of real estate and may lack the practical experience garnered from honing their skills on a regular basis.

When calculating your expense estimates, if you have a mortgage, the money needed to fund your escrow account is bound to increase periodically from rising insurance and taxes. Have you accounted for all the maintenance expenses and utility bills that will come in the mail? Keep in mind you will need to have enough money for the purchase price plus closing costs, plus potential preparation or renovation costs to purchase a property.

Then there is the unexpected to plan for. The very nature of such unexpected expenses meets the definition of the expression. The idea here is not to become cash poor and house rich, you will need money to live too. How much of a lifestyle change are you willing to make if your entertainment budget is transferred into your monthly mortgage expense?

If you are borrowing on an adjustable based mortgage, then your payments will likely fluctuate as well. In the case of an adjustable rate loan you could be the beneficiary of falling rates and that would help your cash flow. Recently, however, we have experienced extremely low interest rates for quite some time and many indicators suggest interest rates are far more likely to rise in the near and long term than they are to fall.

UNDERSTANDING YOUR COSTS

Understanding what your costs are or what they could be is an important part of the planning process. Most of the "extra" costs associated with buying a property are revealed when you apply for a loan. At this point you are exposed to the bank's fees and the *closing costs* that must be paid to purchase the property. **To sum up closing costs in a sentence, add about 7% to the price you have agreed to pay for a property.** This will surely vary based on many factors but know it is not a few hundred dollars, closing costs can be very significant if you are not prepared for them.

CLOSING COSTS

The term closing costs is a catch-all phrase used to categorize some or all the following:

- **Real Estate Taxes** - The portion of real estate taxes you must pay at the closing is usually calculated on a *per diem* basis. If the seller has paid their real estate taxes for some or all the coming year, you must reimburse them at the closing for the difference between the number of days they have used and the number of days you will use. The closing agent will take the annual taxes and divide them by 365 days to determine the per diem tax due. If the seller's taxes have not been paid up to the closing date, you will receive a credit, or the money will be set aside to pay the taxes on your behalf.

- **Escrows** - Sums of money set aside for contingencies are held in an *escrow account*, usually by one of the attorneys. Contingencies would be things which have been agreed to be taken care of, after a closing. Money is set aside to ensure that these things are done, or the escrow money can be used to do it. If your money is placed in escrow, it will not become an expense if it is returned to you.

- **Title Insurance** - A type of insurance policy that covers you if there is a problem with the deed or ownership of the property you purchased. You should buy this when purchasing real estate even if you do not have a loan.

- **Title Search Fees** – These are fees which cover the expense of sending someone to the county clerk's office to inspect the chain of title and ensure there are no problems with the property that would affect the title insurance policy being issued.

- **Fuel Oil** – Home heating oil or propane in tanks is adjusted and the seller usually gets a credit for the unused portion remaining in a tank. It may sound petty, but a 250-gallon oil tank filled at market prices around $3 per gallon could have $750 of oil in it that a seller does not want to pass along to you as a gift.

- **Recording Fees** – These are for the deed or other documents that need to be *recorded* or filed with county and state offices.

- **Your Attorney's Fees** – The fee you agreed upon plus expenses your attorney may have advanced for title searches, surveys or other items required to complete the transaction on your behalf.

- **The Bank's Attorney** – Yes, the bank expects you to pay their attorney to draft and review the loan documents when giving you a mortgage.

- **Loan Costs** – *Loan origination fees* are costs banks charge for *underwriting* or approving a loan for you. *Points* or upfront interest charges to *buy down* or reduce your long-term interest rate are common. Fees and costs for credit reports, appraisals, inspections, surveys, lead-based paint inspections and flood insurance in waterfront or low-lying areas deemed flood zones are additional types of expenses the bank may require you to bear.

- **Other Fees** - Depending on where your property is located, other fees may apply to the transfer of real estate. On a property I sold recently, my buyer was assessed a "preservation fee". Up to $150,000 of the sale price was exempt. The amount of the sale was $200,000, therefore, the sale price of $200,000 minus the $150,000 credit leaves $50,000 taxable at the rate of 2%. This calculation results in a fee to be paid by the buyer of $1,000 in this example.

- **Homeowner's Insurance** – This is insurance, required by lenders, which provides reimbursement to you as an owner for damage to the property and *contents* such as your furnishings, as defined in the policy. The lender is usually named as *an additional insured* on the policy to protect their interests.

- **Mortgage Insurance** – This is a separate type of policy which would pay off a mortgage upon the death or permanent disability of the borrower. Mortgage insurance is usually not required, but you should be aware of its existence. This may be paid from escrows if allowed by the lender.

- **Mortgage Recording Tax** – Some states, about eight according to my research, charge a tax when you record a mortgage. In New York there is a "basic tax of 50 cents per $100 of mortgage debt or obligation secured" plus a "special additional tax of 25 cents per $100 of mortgage debt or obligation secured" plus "an additional tax of 25 cents per $100 of mortgage debt or obligation secured..." and there are some variations and exceptions by city or county. When added up, this could equal a 1% additional tax or $1,000 owed for every $100,000 you borrow as secured money in New York State, so check your local tax codes.

- **Transfer Tax** – A state's surcharge (tax) for buying a home with borrowed money. In New York State, the law is defined in Publication 577 (2/10) and reads: "Tax Law Article 31 imposes a real estate transfer tax on each conveyance of real property, or interest in real property, when the consideration exceeds $500. The tax is computed at a rate of two dollars for each $500 of consideration, or for any fractional part of $500".

- **Mansion Tax** – Another State tax applied to properties sold for more than one million dollars. In New York State, this law is also defined in Publication 577 (2/10) and reads: "An additional tax is imposed on each conveyance of real property or interest in real property used in whole or in part as a personal residence when the consideration for the entire conveyance is $1 million or more. The additional tax is computed at a rate of one percent of the consideration, or part of the consideration, attributable to the residential real property." The law further states the tax is to be <u>paid by the buyer</u> within 15 days.

The preceding list is the buyer's responsibilities. The seller also has closing costs to contend with. Sellers are usually responsible for things like their attorney's fee, realtors' commissions, and transfer taxes. There may be loan *payoff costs* to *satisfy* an existing mortgage and *record* a document known as the *mortgage satisfaction* with the town clerk, so it becomes a matter of public record. The seller may also have expenses to repair items as agreed in the *contract of sale* or uncovered during an inspection that need to be addressed before a closing can occur.

This is not a complete list, but it includes the basics that you will see throughout much of the country. Inquire with realtors or a local attorney to learn more about other charges that may be commonplace in your area.

MORE CLOSING COSTS
I would highly recommend you have an inspection by a qualified builder, architect, or engineer to avoid costly surprises for any property you are

buying. Even though this is not required, it is an expense that often provides lots of information about the property and can give you leverage in negotiating or renegotiating the purchase price based on the examination's findings.

In rare instances, inspections may uncover a deal breaker such as an environmental issue or serious foundation flaw, which may prompt you to back out of a purchase. Obtaining an accurate survey or having one done will confirm you are buying what has been represented to you, or indicate a potential problem, such as the incorrect location of property lines, fences, easements, etc.

Again, in rare cases, a survey might show something as dramatic as a structure which is built too close to or even straddling over a property line. There are well documented cases where builders have built on the wrong property lot, as bizarre as that sounds. These kinds of situations result in *title insurance claims*.

CHAPTER 17
THE CLOSING

The *closing* is a term used to describe a point in time when all parties that have an interest in the transfer of a deed come together to complete the transfer. The deed is a legal document that transfers title or the legal right to own, use and eventually resell a property from one person to another. A period of four to six weeks between contact signing and a closing date should be expected when a mortgage needs to be approved. At the closing, the buyer and seller will settle accounts and pay or reimburse each other for any amounts due. I prefer to call it settlement day.

THE CLOSING TABLE

The place of *closing* is often scheduled at the office of the seller's attorney. A closing can be at a bank, a mortgage broker's office, or anywhere the attorneys and *closing agent* agree to meet. A closing is usually attended by the sellers and their attorney, the buyers and their attorney (If two lawyers are required), a closing agent, one or more real estate brokers (to collect their commission check) and sometimes a representative for the lender. Altogether about eight people will typically gather in the conference room around the *closing table*. Although this may vary depending upon the State you live in.

A closing agent or *escrow agent* typically works for the title company and is an impartial person in a real estate transaction who has the financial responsibility of disbursing funds in escrow, mortgage proceeds and other monies properly and at the same time. Among other things, the closing agent also represents the interests of the lender verifying that all the documents and disclosures required by a lender are properly completed and signed at the closing.

TITLE COMPANY

A *title company* researches the *chain of title* to determine the property you are buying may be transferred to you as a rightful owner. The process is called a *title search* which traces and examines the ownership records as far back as they are recorded, to determine the seller has the legal right to sell you the property. During a title search, judgments, unpaid liens or taxes, mortgages, deed restrictions, covenants, easements or a right of way and other discrepancies may arise. Each of these issues will be addressed and resolved to *clear title.*

The title company will issue a *title insurance policy* which will protect you and your lender, if there is a mortgage, in the event of a future challenge to your ownership or property rights.

Sometimes questions about aliases or identity can arise during a title search which must be resolved before closing. Multiple people with the same name appear in searches and some of them may have outstanding liens. The title company and closing agent need to determine if any of these debts are the seller's responsibility. If issues cannot be resolved to the closing agent's satisfaction at the time of closing, funds may be held in escrow until the issues are clarified or resolved.

The closing agent is also charged with the responsibility of *recording* the deed and mortgage document prepared at the closing with the town clerk. Recording a deed makes it part of the public record and helps to protect you should a claim ever arise as to rightful ownership. *Town clerks* or *recorders* of a deed generally require notarized signatures. Therefore, most title agents are a notary and can attest to your valid signature for recording purposes. This is one of the reasons you are always asked for personal identification at the closing table.

TRANSFER OF FUNDS

Payment is usually expected in the form of a bank wire or by a bank check to guaranty the funds are available and received at the time of closing by the seller. Personal checks in minimal amounts, usually under a few hundred dollars may be accepted to settle open expenses such as a water bill etc.

THE CLOSING STATEMENT

A lot of papers are shuffled around the closing table and you will sign plenty of documents. A fair amount of money also changes hands and there can be multiple debits and credits due to the buyer and seller. Rather than writing checks back and forth, all sums of money due to or from each party are calculated on a *closing statement*. With the assistance of the attorney(s), the closing agent will net out one amount due or owed to each party. The closing agent calculates adjustments, checks that everything balances, then issues checks to each party for the amounts due per the closing statement.

At the closing table, you should check the math on the closing statement yourself and ask as many questions as necessary to understand what you are paying for. Also verify you have received all the credits you are aware of that are due to you. I have seen lawyers make mistakes on behalf of the seller, like not getting credit for a full tank of oil or adjustments previously agreed upon for repairs and so forth. Sometimes adjustments due to either party are not outlined in a contract and you must speak up to ensure they are included on the closing statement during the closing process. There may be opportunities to negotiate some final details, so do not leave any extra money on the table, literally.

Examples of debits and credits found on a closing statement:

> Escrowed deposit for purchase from buyer
>   held by attorney
> Balance of sale price from buyer
>   (Often mortgage proceeds)
> Real estate taxes prepaid by seller
> Fuel oil or propane gas in a tank
> Taxes or fees due from sale of property
> Unpaid real estate taxes
> Broker's sales commission
> Attorney fees
> Title Insurance premium
> Recording fees for documents

SIMULTANEOUS CLOSINGS

When the purchase of one property is contingent upon the sale of another, and the timing of the purchase and sale align, both properties may be closed upon at virtually the same time and the title clerk will record them together. This is known as a *simultaneous closing*.

CERTIFICATES OF OCCUPANCY

Certificates of Occupancy, or *CO's*, must be valid when purchasing a property. Therefore, this should be a requirement in your contract as noted in chapter seven, "Making an Offer". Most sellers will simply transfer the documents they received when they bought the property. However, if new alterations to the property or structures on it such as an expansion, adding a garage, finishing a basement etc. were completed without obtaining the proper permits and updating the CO, you could be facing a huge delay in closing until the paperwork is updated.

CO's and similar documents can take months or years to acquire if there are underlying problems and can cost significant sums of money to attain. In rare instances where work performed is deemed to be illegal, this may void an existing CO. Under these circumstances, it may be impossible to get a new CO without removing the changes that were made. If the seller does not have a valid CO or other document used in your area to allow occupancy, this should be a deal breaker.

All cash deals, owner financing or using third-party lenders are ways in which properties without valid CO's, or CO's that do not cover everything you are buying, can be transferred from a seller to a buyer.

As an example, consider I spent fourteen months getting an updated CO for my personal residence in preparation for selling it. This occurred because of an original deck that came with the house that was not listed on the original CO, which was some thirty years old. Even though the deck was on the original building plans that were approved by the town, the town required new plans, inspections, and changes to the construction of the deck before I could obtain a proper CO for the deck.

Obtaining a new CO may also have tax consequences when you update a property and the town re-assesses the real estate taxes based on improvements that were never included in the original valuation calculations for tax purposes.

A town might even impose penalties for this. The town may also have the right to request other updates before issuing a CO if their inspection uncovers additional code violations in or on your property.

If you have no experience in this area you will likely find it to be a very frustrating experience. Most people use an expediter to speed up the permit filing process, but since most people use an expediter, the process is not truly faster. However, it could still be worthwhile to use an expediter, who can reduce errors that might cause extra delays outside the normal submission process.

OTHER OCCUPANCY CERTIFICATES

Other certificates, such as a *Certificate of Use* or a *Certificate of Compliance*, may be issued by a local governing authority. Regardless of the format of the certificate, if this is the traditional method of certifying a property is in good order, and the certificate meets the current codes for occupancy, then it will be enough for your purposes.

If a property does not have a CO, and there is an existing violation, you could be required to file for and obtain a CO. A variance is an exception to a building code that permits a previously unpermitted use to exist. In these situations, simply applying for a building permit to rectify the violation will not suffice.

Common situations requiring variances occur where the setback or distance from the property line is less than the minimum required by a code for a garage to be constructed. A garage that was built to close to a property line, deemed to be a violation, could be allowed to remain in place if a variance is granted. The garage would then be included on the CO. If the variance application were denied, the garage would have to be moved or removed.

Upon applying for a variance, you would have to notify surrounding property owners to attend a public hearing in which your application will be reviewed and input from the community is invited. The complicated nature of applying for a variance, the specific requirements that must be met and the fact that a favorable outcome is not guaranteed, make avoiding this pitfall important whenever possible.

THE FOLLOW UP

The attorney(s) will provide each party with a settlement statement outlining the debits and credits due or owed to each party for record keeping purposes. You will want to make a copy of these for your accountant as this will have an impact on your tax return, since many of the items you are paying for may be tax deductible.

CHAPTER 18
PREPARING TO MOVE

CONGRATULATIONS!
Once you have a contract to purchase a property you can get a head start on your moving preparations by making a detailed list of everything that needs to be accomplished and highlight the items that can be addressed before the closing. Please note that none of these advance undertakings should cost you any money. You should not commit to paying for anything until you do close on a property, because things can and do happen that delay or kill contracts from time to time.

You will take possession of a vacant home, so if scheduling permits consider doing any major work, painting, carpet cleaning or floor refinishing because it will go much easier and more quickly before you move in. And it will get done, because if you are a procrastinator, it may not get done after you move in as other priorities may arise.

Depending upon the condition of your property you might be calling a contractor to do renovations or be handling it yourself. The more you can do on your own, the more you will save and the more sweat equity you will accrue. If you are going to hire a professional, try to work with the seller to arrange appointments for estimates from contractors to view the property if you have not already done this as part of your planning to make the purchase.

If you have not been in direct contact with the seller, then you may have to work through your broker to set up appointments. You can save time and money if you are able to start work immediately upon closing and not lose weeks trying to select a contractor or getting them to schedule you in. As the closing date nears, if it looks firm, you should start scheduling tentative work whenever possible, on the premise it is easier to reschedule than it is to get on the schedule of a busy contractor in the first place.

MOVING COMPANY

Use the time between signing your contract and the closing to hire a moving company if you are not planning on moving yourself or with the help of family and friends. Allow enough lead time to check references and pricing. I can tell you from experience movers are very busy the last two or three days of the month and the first two or three days because most tenants move on or about the end of the month in addition to homeowners. Scheduling weekday moves instead of weekends is likely to get you a much better rate as well.

Asking the mover when they can give you the best rate rather than giving them a hard date might work for you. In some areas the time of the year also impacts pricing as I have experienced in New York to Florida moves where snowbirds migrate regularly. Many people want to be in a new home before the school season or holiday season starts to make for smoother transitions.

Ask if the mover is licensed and insured. Call the *Better Business Bureau* to find out if a mover has had any complaints and how they were handled. Do they have any online reviews that will indicate how they have performed for others? Obviously, you will want to avoid a mover with an unreasonable number of complaints.

When the mover comes to give you an estimate, ask if anything appears problematic and if there are any items they will not take to avoid last minute surprises. Ask how far in advance they are booked. Some movers may sell packing supplies, but you might want to shop around for competitive pricing or visit the local grocery stores to pick up free boxes because you will need plenty of them.

INTERSTATE MOVING
If you are making a move to another state, your mover should have a USDOT number that appears on their estimate and in their ads. Interstate movers are subject to licensing and registration by

the Federal Motor Carrier Administration. An interstate mover should inform you of restrictions you might have to consider. Do some research on your own as well.

You should not pack food or liquids to avoid infestation and leaks that can damage your possessions. Some states regulate types of plants they allow. You will probably need to re-register your vehicles, change your driver's license and re-register to vote in addition to the other preparations for moving that are discussed in this section.

REDUCE WHAT YOU HAVE TO MOVE
Movers will consider the time, value and volume of items they must move when they calculate an estimate for you. Reducing the volume of what you move will have a direct impact on the cost of your move. Consider selling, donating or disposing of items you may never use. Garage sales, Craigslist and other sites are great ways to turn unwanted items into some extra cash at a time when it probably can be most helpful.

LABEL EVERYTHING
It is a good idea to label everything to be moved with the location it is going to. Just because it is coming out of your current kitchen doesn't mean it is going into the new kitchen, you may want to store it in the basement or garage. A marker will do if you don't mind doing a lot of writing.

When my wife and I moved, she printed very large labels for each room, the garage and the basement. The labels were easy to read and were placed in the upper right corner on each side of every box. On moving day about eight movers showed up and the outgoing move was easy. The move into the new house went very smoothly too and it was easy to verify everything was put into the right location. This eliminated the need for us to do a lot of extra lifting.

We also used large bright colored FRAGILE and HEAVY stickers to identify boxes that required a little extra care. Even though you may have found a good moving company, sometimes their employees do not all exercise the same level of care and the bright stickers allowed us to keep an eye on things as they came off the truck. If you want to be super organized, you can number each box by room and create an inventory list for each box. If you don't expect to unpack everything quickly a numbering system will help you find specific items when you need them relatively easily.

Since our move was a relatively large one that required five moving trucks, organization was very helpful. The basement labels were further designated with large numbers to indicate zones. The zone system allowed us to sort and keep similar items together.

IMPORTANT ITEMS

Pack the things that are most valuable or important to you that size permits in a carry-on travel bag and take them with you rather than entrusting them to the mover. Keep some basic tools handy as well. If you have pets, will they require any special attention? Will you need to plan for boarding or meals during the move?

Transport your own medications, jewelry and very important papers. This becomes extremely important if you are doing a move that may require your belongings to be stored during a move when there is a gap between moving from one location to another. Pack enough necessities such as clothes, toiletries and sleepwear for a few days depending on your moving circumstances. How important will it be to get your hands on your coffee maker in the morning?

On my last move, my wife and I spent five days in a hotel because we had to be out of the house we were living in before we could move into the one we were buying. The deal we struck made it worth while for us to bear this inconvenience and packing intelligently made it comfortable for us.

FLOOR PLAN

Ask the seller if they have a floor plan or measure the rooms so you can determine if your major pieces of furniture will fit and where you might want to locate them. This will also make the mover's job easier and save time leaving you less work after the movers are gone. Do not assume your furniture will fit through the doors or make it through the type of turns that may make it difficult or impossible to get large pieces into the room where you want them.

UTILITIES INSURANCE & MORE

You will need a homeowner's insurance policy in place prior to closing which may have to meet certain requirements set by the lender. The utilities will also have to be transferred into your name. Many people contact the utilities after the closing, but you can call up to a few weeks prior to the closing and schedule the transfer, this will avoid delays and the date can easily be rescheduled if your closing date is pushed back for any reason. Avoiding disconnection of existing services will save you the reconnection fee most utilities charge.

Sometimes the transfer can be accomplished with a phone call, but if you have not had an account with the utility company or have weak credit you may be asked to visit their offices to fill out an application and leave a security deposit. Basic things that might be on your list to address are electric, gas, oil, cable, internet, alarms, water etc. You might also want to schedule disconnect dates for the home or apartment you are relocating from.

Forward your mail, which you can do online at USPS.com in advance of your closing. Remember to send out change of address information to all your family and friends plus subscriptions, banking and other bills.

SAFETY EQUIPMENT & MORE

Smoke detectors should be installed in bedrooms and hallways. CO detectors should be installed in areas near any heat source. Placing a fire extinguisher in the kitchen, garage or any place where flammable materials would be stored is a good idea. Locate the water main and become familiar with your electric panel. Make sure you know how to operate any pumps or generators that may be present.

Try to avoid leaving the house you have just purchased vacant for an extended period. If you must do so, then here are some considerations you should be aware of. The first thing you should always do is change the locks, so you know who has keys to the house.

Vacant properties create increased risks of vandalism, theft, and other problems. You may incur more maintenance costs for exterior upkeep or utility costs, especially in colder regions where heat must be maintained, or a property needs to be winterized to protect against freezing pipes and water damage. In hot regions, no air conditioning can cause mold issues. Unchecked leaks that arise from any source, including neighboring units if you have a multi-unit home or an attached unit such as a condominium or co-op, can cause considerable damage if no one is aware of the problem.

Infestation of insects such as fleas, roaches and vermin or animals that make homes in vacant properties can cause damage and will result in additional extermination or repair costs.

INSURANCE AND CANCELLATIONS
Insurance companies may send an inspector out to visit your home. In my experience they always notify you and they rarely want to come inside. The purpose of the visit is to verify the address and document the size and condition of the exterior of the house with photos and a visual inspection. You will typically receive a follow up letter and it may indicate items needing attention such as a loose railing.

If you are not planning on moving in reasonably quickly after closing on your new home let your insurance agent know. **Your insurance company does not want to cover vacant property for any extended period, which could prompt a cancellation notice you might not be prepared for.** You will have some time to move in, usually thirty days, but not much more once you are on their radar. When I work on houses that remain vacant for an extended period, my insurance company requires me to pay for a construction policy. This type of policy is much more expensive than my regular homeowner's policy and usually only covers a shorter term of three to six months.

CHAPTER 19
SELLING

Eventually there will come a time when you may want to sell your home. As we learned in the buying process, if a Certificate of Occupancy or other required document is not available, months could be lost trying to obtain these documents, adding long term delays to your closing. The same holds true when you are selling.

Is your paperwork in order? When buying you might be willing to wait for the paperwork if you found a bargain, but when selling you could easily lose a potential buyer that cannot afford to wait for you to get your paperwork in order. Your buyer may need to relocate before you are ready to close a deal for a myriad of reasons, or could lose their financing, as most mortgage commitments have expiration dates that are only a few weeks long.

Therefore, from the first moment you consider selling or just as a practical matter, make sure there are no changes such as additions to the primary structure or add-ons such as garages, sheds, greenhouses etc. which are not shown on the survey.

A missing deed is usually an easy fix if it was recorded properly when a property was purchased, and no changes have been made that would affect the deed. If the deed cannot be located, a property owner can obtain certified copies from the Town Clerk's office where it was originally filed.

Obtaining a duplicate Certificate of Occupancy or similar document can also be an easy task if no changes were made. You can do this by visiting your local town or county building department. The building department will have a copy on record or tell you how to obtain copies of the documents you need. If you have made changes, the building department will walk you through the steps their authority requires you to take to obtain an updated document.

Please note, you may also have to get approval from agencies or departments other than the building department such as the fire department, planning department etc. to obtain an updated CO. Inquire early in the processes to determine everything that is needed. Many of the requirements from different departments can be addressed simultaneously rather than consecutively and this can save you weeks or months of time.

Receiving incomplete or inaccurate information can be a tremendous source of frustration when dealing with multiple authorities. It is a good idea to confirm the information you receive with another source or town employee whenever possible and always ask; "Is there anything else I need to do or know?"

A survey is not always required by a buyer in a cash deal or with third party financing, even though they should insist upon you providing one. If there is a bank involved in the transaction, they will require a survey. If you provide a survey and it is deemed to be outdated, illegible or problematic by the lender for some reason, the buyer may have to bear the cost of updating your survey to satisfy the bank.

For these reasons, when I am the buyer, I like to make my offers and contracts subject to the seller providing an updated survey and CO's to control my costs.

PREPARING A PROPERTY TO SELL

Staging a property is preparing it to sell by making it look more attractive to potential buyers. A furnished home may need some de-cluttering or accessories to make it more appealing to potential buyers and a vacant home may need to be furnished to maximize its potential selling price. Some sellers rent furniture to create a lived in, comfortable appearance.

DO YOU HAVE A TENANT?

If you have a multi-family home with one or more tenants, are the tenants staying or going when you sell? You can sell a property with a tenant subject to the new owner assuming the lease or you might decide to terminate the tenancy before you list the property. This would allow you to offer the entire property in vacant and ready to move in condition.

If you are locked into a long-term lease with a tenant, then your options would be to sell to a buyer willing to take the property with your tenant or making a deal with your tenant to break the lease.

If you have a month to month lease with a tenant or a *holdover* tenant, and the lease has expired, but the tenant is still paying rent, you can give them a 30-day notice to vacate. Then you would have to start an eviction proceeding if necessary to take back the premises if they have not moved out.

THE FINAL WORD

To restate part of the first paragraph of the Prologue in this book...

There Is More To Know, Than There Is To Do!

It is important to understand that you have learned a lot about potential issues you may never have to face, which clearly is not the same thing as experiencing all the challenges or setbacks discussed in this book. I trust you have found some useful information and/or ideas within this writing that will help you find the perfect home. My wish is that you have become inspired and will be motivated to fulfill your own dreams and experience all the joy life has to offer, with just enough challenges along the way to appreciate the difference.

DISCLAIMER

This section is the liability disclaimer portion of the book. I am not a tax professional or an attorney, I am a real estate investor. My specific experience is in single family homes and small commercial properties. I wrote this book to share some of my successes and mistakes with you so that you might have a better chance of buying the right home for you the first time. Whether you already own a home or are considering buying your first home, there are many potential pitfalls this writing can help you avoid simply by being aware they exist.

Accounting for real estate transactions can be a very complex matter requiring an experienced accountant. You should seek an accountant that has specific experience with real estate and understands the many nuances of properly preparing your tax returns. A true professional remains abreast of the constant changes in the tax code that can affect their clients. The extra money you might spend here for the right person to represent you can pay dividends in the form of more accurate accounting and less potential tax problems down the road. Here your best defense is a good offense.

Yes, most professionals can conduct research to find the answers they need for your questions, but as my mother always told me, if you do not know what questions to ask, how will you get the advice you need? Therefore, you should rely on professionals to make you aware of your responsibilities and to discuss or mitigate risks you may become exposed to.

Any information or advice contained within this writing is for informational purposes and should not be relied upon when addressing your tax responsibilities. This information is meant to make you aware of some of the potential tax implications you may not have been previously aware of. ALWAYS check with an accounting professional for advice because every individual's tax liability is different, the tax codes are complex, often subject to interpretation and are ever changing.

Please also be informed that any discussion relating to U.S. Federal and/or State tax responsibilities contained in this book is not intended or written to be used, and cannot be used, for the purposes of (i) preparing your taxes (ii) avoiding penalties under the Internal Revenue Code or (iii) promoting, marketing, or recommending to another party any transaction or matter addressed herein.

Highly Recommended
Real Estate Accountant
(My Brothers Firm):

Borneman & Associates CPA, P.C.

Certified Public Accountants
Financial, Business & Tax Advisors
17 Conklin Street, Suite 3
Farmingdale, NY 11735

James Borneman

Phone: 516-864-0770

SPEAKING ENGAGEMENTS

The author is available for speaking engagements and individual consultations.

Email: RobertBorneman7@gmail.com
Facebook.com/RobertBorneman7

Also by the author:

Available at.Amazon.com as a download in digital
format and in a printed paperback version.
Search for the title or my name.
You can also email me to purchase a copy at:
RobertBorneman7@gmail.com

Also by the author:

Available at.Amazon.com as a download in digital
format and in a printed paperback version.
Search for the title or my name.
You can also email me to purchase a copy at:
RobertBorneman7@gmail.com

Screenplay and full-length feature film

written by Robert Borneman:

SNAPSHOT

Winner – Manhattan Film Festival
"Best Social Issue in a Feature Film"

Starring Zach McGowan, Joyce DeWitt, Michael Pare, Angela Gots, David Chokachi, Martin Kove, Nina Transfeld, Michael Rivera, Angela Little and Robert Loggia

U.S. Distribution: Osiris Entertainment
Foreign Distribution: Fabrication Films

www.ingramcontent.com/pod-product-compliance
Lightning Source LLC
Chambersburg PA
CBHW071254220526
45468CB00001B/128